D1546371

Henry James and the Dramatic Analogy

HENRY JAMES
AND
THE DRAMATIC ANALOGY

A Study of the Major Novels

of the Middle Period

by

Joseph Wiesenfarth, F.S.C.

FORDHAM UNIVERSITY PRESS • NEW YORK

For Mother, Charles and Marge

ACKNOWLEDGMENTS

Leon Edel for *The Selected Letters of Henry James,* ed. Leon Edel, copyright 1955 by Leon Edel. Published by Farrar, Straus and Cudahy.

Oxford University Press for *The Notebooks of Henry James,* ed. F. O. Matthiessen and Kenneth B. Murdock, copyright 1947.

Charles Scribner's Sons for quotations from *The Letters of Henry James,* edited by Percy Lubbock;

The Art of the Novel, Critical Prefaces by Henry James, with an Introduction by Richard P. Blackmur (Copyright 1934, Charles Scribner's Sons, renewal copyright 1962);

"In The Cage," *What Maisie Knew, The Awkward Age* from *The Novels and Tales of Henry James* (Copyright 1908, Charles Scribner's Sons, renewal copyright 1936, Henry James).

Rutgers University Press for *The Scenic Art: Notes on Acting and Drama: 1872-1901,* by Henry James, ed., with an introduction and notes, by Allan Wade, copyright 1948.

Contents

Preface

In a craftsman-to-craftsman statement in a letter to Paul Bourget, Henry James remarked that "questions of art and form . . . interest me deeply—really much more than any other; and so, not less, do they interest you: yet, though they frequently come up between us . . . I nowadays never seem to see you long enough at once to thresh them comfortably out with you." Just four years later, on September 9, 1902, James reiterated his interest in the problems of the writer's craft in a note to his Rye neighbor Ford Madox Ford: "Nothing . . . is ever more interesting to me than the consideration, with those who care to see, or want to, of these bottomless questions of How, and Why and Whence and What . . . in connection with the mystery of one's Craft." It is with this Henry James, absorbed in the novel with the dedicated interest of a painstaking maker, that this book is concerned. It discusses questions of How and Why and Whence and What with those who, like Bourget and Ford, are no less interested in such questions than was James himself.

Henry James and the Dramatic Analogy is a study of James's theory of the dramatic novel and of the application of that theory in an analysis and evaluation of four major novels of his middle period: *The Spoils of Poynton, What Maisie Knew, The Awkward Age,* and *The Sacred Fount.* The first chapter suggests how the term *dramatic novel* raises a problem in literary theory which must be solved if James's middle— and late—novels are adequately to be appreciated. Subsequently, in the same chapter, a solution in terms of an analogy between the novel and the drama is proposed. In brief, it is suggested that James recognized "intensity," "economy," and "objectivity" as indispensable qualities in the play and that he attempted to incorporate these qualities into a novel which he conceived of as "dramatized." This theory entails a discussion of five specific elements of James's dramatized narrative: language, action, scene, picture, and centre. It is proposed that through a careful use of these elements James achieved the qualities of "intensity," "objectivity," and "economy" and thus effected a dramatic novel. The study then passes to an analysis and evaluation of *Poynton, Maisie,* and the *Age* as dramatic novels. Since James referred specifically to the "intensity" of *The Spoils of Poynton,* the "economy" of *What Maisie Knew,* and the "objectivity" of *The Awkward Age,* these qualities are given major attention in the discussion of these respective novels. The last chapter attempts to place and evaluate the problematical *Sacred Fount* in relation to the tradition of the dramatic novel; this chapter also demonstrates the relation of all four novels to the "major phase."

Critics and scholars have not entirely neglected the study of the dramatic nature of James's novels, as is made evident by the recognition accorded the scholarship of Beach, Lubbock, Short, Fergusson, and Edel in the text and notes of the first chapter. Beach has raised the problems of time and representation, Lubbock has studied point of view, Short has minutely examined the meaning of important terms, Fergusson has studied the similarity of development in the action of the play and the Jamesian novel, and Edel has provided a thorough study of James as a playwright. The notes to the chapters on the particular novels discussed in this book indicate, argue with, and evaluate the contributions of these and other critics to an understanding of *Poynton, Maisie,* the *Age,* and the

Fount. Though I sometimes find myself in disagreement with others, I have chosen for the sake of a coherent exposition of ideas to skirmish in my notes, not my text. The reader interested in this variety of academic excitement is referred to the back of the book. Suffice it to say here that no critic has treated the novels in relation to a developed theory of James's dramatic novel. In both the speculative and practical areas of literary study, there is available neither a complete theory of James's dramatic novel nor a complete study of any one of these novels of the middle period as a dramatic novel that prepares for the later novels and stands transitionally between the late and early periods of James's development.

The intent and purpose of this book, consequently, is to supply a rationale for James's novels from 1897 to 1904—for the "minor" and "major" phases—and in light of that rationale to evaluate the novels from 1897 to 1901 in terms of their literary structure. Whereas some attention has been given to this phase of James's career (notably in the recent books of Oscar Cargill and D. W. Jefferson) and in an encouraging way demonstrates a renewed interest in a relatively neglected area of James's development, insufficient work has been done to provide for a theoretical understanding of his middle novels and an evaluation of their merit and position of influence by esthetic norms. To these ends the following pages are offered.

With an emphasis not usual with him, James once wrote: "I *am* damned critical—for it's the only thing to be, and all else is damned humbug." To the extent that this book has eschewed any such humbug, it is indebted to the conscientious help I have been given by many hands. To Professor James Hafley of The Catholic University of America, then, I take this occasion to acknowledge my appreciation for his many readings of the manuscript, for his criticism of its content, and especially for his encouragement and kindness to me. To his colleagues, Professors Richard Foley and Francis Litz, for their suggestion of certain helpful amendments, I am indebted. For a stimulating insight into *The Awkward Age,* I am thankful to Professor Craig La Drière of The Catholic University. To Professor Marius Bewley of Fordham University, for his helpful reading of the manuscript in an early draft, I am grateful. I wish to thank Professor Leon Edel of New York University for two letters which established certitude for me in some matters that would otherwise have remained problematical. I am grateful to Edwin A. Quain, S.J., and Miss Donna Thomas of Fordham University Press for their many services and especially for their attention to galleys and page-proofs. To my confreres at De La Salle College, Washington, D. C., and to my colleagues and confreres at La Salle College, Philadelphia, I express my gratitude for their services, their interest, and their support. To these helpers and the many others who with them have made this work possible, I acknowledge my debt and express my appreciation.

The dramatic form seems to me the most beautiful thing possible; the misery of the thing is that the baseness of the English-speaking stage affords no setting for it.

—HENRY JAMES
Paris, 1882

1

The Dramatic Novel: Its Qualities and Elements

In origin, the problem of a dramatic narrative is as ancient as literary speculation itself. Plato's *Republic* makes this evident in that passage which records the speech of Socrates to the novice Adeimantus:

> . . . I think I can now make clear what was not plain before, that poetry and mythology sometimes appear as complete imitations [plays] . . . and sometimes as narratives of the poet himself. . . . The mixture of the two methods you find in the works of the epic poets and in many other places.[1]

And Aristotle echoes Plato in the *Poetics* when he discusses the possible manners of imitation:

> . . . One may either (1) speak at one moment in the narrative and at another in an assumed character, as Homer does; or (2) one may remain the same throughout, without any such change; or (3) the imitators may represent the whole story dramatically, as though they were actually doing the things described.[2]

Now Henry James clearly recognized this difference between the form of the drama and that of the novel, and his occasional conversion of a novel into a play makes this evident.[3] Indeed, James was quite as aware of the impossibility of having a novel that is a drama as Plato and Aristotle were incapable of conflating the form of Homer with that, say, of Sophocles. The distinction between forms based on voice structure was and is as familiar to modern theoreticians as it was to the Greeks, and the former no more than the latter thought to confuse them. James, however, more impressionist than formalist, had a penchant for speaking of the novel in terms of the drama, and he thus favored the ambiguous, though analogous, midpoint of *dramatic novel*. But for James the problem of writing a novel which would have those qualities that he associated with the drama was obviously not one turning on his ignorance of the forms in question. In fact it was James's working familiarity with both forms that led him to speak of the novel in terms of the drama.

Critics and scholars who have tried to compose James's theory of the dramatic novel from the scattered pieces of his theoretical, critical, and creative writings have, by and large, worked to pictures similar to those presented by Joseph Warren Beach and Edwin Marion Snell. "I like to distinguish between novelists that *tell* and those that *show*," writes Beach, "and when I say that James was a dramatic storyteller, I mean that he was one of those that show through scenes."[4] Snell, who serves as a source for Beach's gloss, contends that the reader "must *see* what is happening; it must never (in theory) be outlined or explained—hence James's extension, into the smallest detail, of the technique of the dramatist."[5] These, of course, are fundamentally sound statements, but it is the nature of such generalizations to lack in particularity. It happens that, in this case, the particulars are essential to James's theory and practice of the dramatic novel.

The immediately recognizable virtue in the two statements quoted, nevertheless, lies in their stress on the representational nature of Jamesian fiction. The impression of seeing the action happen rather than hearing it reported is the primary and most important aspect of the dramatic novel, but it is not the only one. James was ever insistent upon the *qualities* of a dramatic novel, and he realized these qualities in his novels by the application of certain techniques (and not the scenic alone).[6] Therefore any rounded understanding of the Jamesian conception of the dramatic novel involves all the qualities and techniques that he continually associated with the novel which represented, exhibited, showed an action.

The representational nature of the dramatic novel is itself only an aspect of the dramatic quality of "intensity," which, together with "objectivity" and "economy," comprises a Jamesian triad of dramatic qualities that exist in both the dramatic novel and the play and form the basis of an analogy between the two forms.

That James indeed associated these qualities of "intensity," "objectivity," and "economy" with the drama and that he continually praised it in terms of them is evident from his many essays on the theatre. He lauded "intensity" as "the Dramatist's all in all," [7] and hailed the acted play as "a novel intensified."[8] The "guarded objectivity" of the play struck James as its "divine Distinction" and "greater than any other,"[9] because he regarded the drama as "the most detached and most impersonal of literary forms."[10] In praise of economic treatment James pronounced *Hedda Gabler* remarkable for its "admirable closeness,"[11] while he considered *Ghosts* "extraordinarily compact and vivid."[12] Ibsen himself, in fact, was saluted as a master of the dramatic form: "for those who care in general for the form that he practices he will always remain one of the talents that have understood it best and exacted most from it, have effected most neatly the ticklish transfusion of life."[13] James time and again praised the Norwegian playwright for the same dramatic qualities that he demanded of his own novels. He wrote of Ibsen's "intensity, his vividness" as part of the "hard compulsion of his strangely inscrutable art."[14] He singled out for special notice the "dramatist's art . . . producing an intensity of interest by means incorruptibly quiet."[15] He thought that Ibsen caught and held one's interest because he addressed himself "so substantially to representation."[16] And, as if to reduce his admiration to essential statement, James wrote large the playwright's "intensity," "economy," and "objectivity" in a single passage on *John Gabriel Borkman:*

> The author . . . arrives at the dramatist's goal—he arrives for all his meagreness at *intensity*. The meagreness, which is after all but an unconscious, an admirable *economy,* never interferes with that: it plays straight into the hands of his rare mastery of form. . . . In the *cold fixed light* of it [the form] the notes that we speak of as deficiencies take a sharp value in the picture.[17]

When James thought of the novel, then, in terms of the drama, it was natural for him to characterize the dramatic novel in terms which applied especially to the play. It was all the more characteristic for him to use these terms with reference to his post-theatrical novels since they followed upon his earlier experience in writing plays. Indeed, it was in these works that James demonstrated that he had at last acquired the "key that, working in the same *general* way, fits the complicated chambers of both the dramatic and narrative lock. . . ."[18] The certainty of this is attested, as Matthiessen and Murdock point out, by *The Spoils of Poynton* and *What Maisie Knew,* which "form the pivotal point between his early and late methods."

> He spoke, while outlining the *Spoils,* of the valuable economy of "fundamental statement." His plays had taught him how to work out what he now called a "close, clear, full scenario"; and for *Maisie* in particular he thought of his structure as a succession of acts.[19]

But it was not only the act of the play but the very qualities of the drama itself that James emulated in his conception of

4

the dramatic novel and that he returned to again and again in his ruminations on the art of dramatizing that novel.

A. QUALITIES

1. *Intensity*

James was simultaneously thinking of Richardson's *Clarissa* and the Théâtre Français when he wrote: "an acted play is a novel intensified...."[20] His delight was not Gray's, whose "idea of heaven was to lie all day on a sofa and read novels. He, poor man, spoke while *Clarissa Harlowe* was still the fashion, and a novel was synonymous with an eternity."[21] James did not conceive of the novel in terms of *Clarissa* and eternity, but rather in terms of the theatre and intensity. For him "the dramatic" was "the sum of all intensities,"[22] and intensity was "the grace to which the enlightened story-teller will at any time, for his interest, sacrifice if need be all other graces,"[23] because a "novel is in its broadest definition a personal, a direct impression of life: that to begin with, constitutes its value, which is greater or less according to the intensity of the impression."[24]

As far as it is possible to specify the meaning of the word *intensity* from the many ways he uses it, James seems to consider a novel to possess the quality of intensity when: (1) it has a carefully and minutely related structure of events which parallel and contrast with each other so as continuously to highlight the meaning of similar and opposite events in an action; (2) events in the novel are in some way observed by the reader and not witnessed to by the guarantees of characters who merely say that they took place, and the language of the novel is itself concrete so as to show (rather than abstract so as to tell) in order to emphasize action, character, and setting in so far as emphasis is possible; and (3) the incidents in the novel involve a personal conflict which reflects and makes prominent intellectual judgments, moral choices and emotional states of one or a few of the more important characters. When each of these dimensions of intensity exists in the highest degree that the subject allows, the novel for James, as will be subsequently seen, in all probability possesses the quality of intensity as an ideal.

There are, then, three dimensions to the quality of intensity as James employs the term. One dimension depends primarily on the extent of structural harmony, and for convenience will be called structural intensity. A second dimension is involved with the vividness of the representation of an action, and will be called representational intensity. The third dimension directly depends on the degree of awareness of a Jamesian agent, and will be called psychological intensity. Since there seems to be no adequate synonym for *intensity*, when intensity is referred to without any qualifying adjective or when it appears unqualified by the context in which it occurs, the reference will be to the quality in all its dimensions —structural, representational, and psychological.

Touching on structural intensity in *The American*, James noted that the "greatest intensity may be arrived at evidently —when the sacrifice of community, of 'related' sides of situations, has not been too rash."[25] He believed that a dangerous loss of intensity was effected by the writer who cut the cable from the balloon of experience, because "from the moment that cable is cut" he was "at large and unrelated."[26] According to James, an intensity was viable in *The Awkward Age* only through a network of relations: "the references in one's action can only be, with intensity, to each other. . . . We are shut up wholly to cross-relations, relations all within the action itself; no part of which is related to anything but some other part— save of course by the relation of the total to life."[27] A structural neatness which disallows loose ends and relates each thing

6

to the other produced for James that structural intensity in fiction which approached the compactness of the drama. "The play," he wrote, "consents to the logic of but one way, mathematically right, and with the loose end as gross an impertinence on its surface, and as grave a dishonour, as the dangle of a snippet of silk or wool on the right side of a tapestry."[28]

James's great concern for representational intensity is evident from his repeated references to the reader's impression of experiencing something for himself. Balzac was to be admired for his ability to use detail to represent his subject: "He squeezes it till it cries, we hardly know whether for pleasure or pain."[29] An incident or even an idea could not be stated; it had to be shown. "No theory is kind to us that cheats us of *seeing*," James remarked to Stevenson.[30] For James, then, "platitude of statement" was "a deplorable depth at any time . . . for any master of representation to sink to. . . ."[31] For this reason he admired Turgenev, who never sank: "an idea, with him, is such and such an individual, with such a hat and waistcoat, bearing the same relation to it as the look of a printed word does to its meaning."[32] The supreme proclamation of representational intensity, however, came some thirty years after this profession of admiration for Turgenev. It appears in the preface to *The Tragic Muse:*

> . . . Processes, periods, intervals, stages, degrees, connexions, may be easily enough and barely enough named, may be unconvincingly stated, in fiction, to the deep discredit of the writer, but it remains the very deuce to represent them, especially represent them under strong compression and in brief and subordinate terms; and this even though the novelist who doesn't represent, and represent "all the time," is lost, exactly as much lost as the painter who, at his work and given his intention, doesn't paint "all the time."[33]

7

And in the preface to "The Altar of the Dead," James restates his preference for representational intensity and relates it to structural intensity. The passage also introduces a third notion of intensity—one intimately related to the agent's sensibility.

> With the preference I have noted for the "neat" evocation—the image, of any sort, with fewest attendant vaguenesses and cheapnesses, fewest loose ends dangling and fewest features missing, the image kept in fine the most susceptible of intensity—with this predilection, I say, the safest arena for the play of moving accidents and mighty mutations and strange encounters, or whatever odd matters, is the field, as I may call it, rather of their second than of their first exhibition. By which to avoid obscurity, I mean nothing more cryptic than I feel myself show them best by showing almost exclusively the way they are felt, by recognizing as their main interest some impression strongly made by them and intensely received.[34]

It is precisely because of his awareness of the psychological dimension represented by the intensely received impression that, while on the one hand, James was displeased with Daudet's *Sappho* and could write the author that "En un mot, ne se passe peut-être pas assez dans l'âme et dans la conscience de Jean,"[35] on the other, he was pleased with those sections of *The Portrait of a Lady* which, because of the fine sensibility of Isabel Archer, show a "maximum of intensity with a minimum of strain."[36] He naturally postulated that for characters in a fiction, "their being finely aware—as Hamlet and Lear, say, are finely aware—makes absolutely the intensity of their adventure, gives the maximum of sense to what befalls them."[37] And following this premise James firmly adopted the position that "the figures in any picture, the agents in any drama, are interesting only in proportion as they feel their respective situation. . . ."[38] Because others "feel without seeing" while Fleda Vetch "both sees and feels," they "minister, at a particular crisis, to the intensity of the free spirit engaged with them."[39] When James failed to project a scene of "A London Life" in relation to the highly sensitive Laura Wing, he charged himself with a "lapse from artistic dignity"[40] because the novel's "intensity ruefully drops."[41]

The importance of intensity as a dramatic quality is evident, as these instances witness, and it is not to be wondered at that James spoke of it both early and laudably in his prefaces, writing that "Since one is dealing with an Action one might borrow a scrap from the Dramatist's all in all, his intensity—which the novelist so ruefully envies him as a fortune in itself."[42]

2. Objectivity

Of objectivity, the second quality of the dramatic novel, James wrote, "I adore a rounded objectivity, a completely and patiently achieved one. . . ."[43] And some fourteen years before he made that remark in a 1913 letter to H. G. Wells, he had written in a similar vein to Mrs. Humphry Ward, who was then in the process of writing her novel *Eleanor*. She had exchanged letters with James and asked for his criticism of the novel as far as it had progressed. His response of July 26, 1899, one interesting for a variety of reasons, is remarkable especially in its plea for objectivity in the novel. He wrote:

> I hold the artist must (infinitely!) know how he is doing it [writing a novel], or he is not doing it at all. I hold he must have a perception of the interests of his subject that grasps him as in a vise, and that (the subject being of course formulated in his mind) he sees the ways that comparatively give it away. And he must there choose and stick and be consistent—and that is the hard-and-fastness and the vise. I am afraid I do differ with you if you mean

9

that the picture can get any *objective* unity from any other source than that; can get it from, e.g., the "personality of the author." From the personality of the author (which, however enchanting, is a thing for the reader only, and not for the author himself, without humiliating abdications, to my sense, to count it at all) it can get nothing but a unity of execution and tone. There is no short cut for the subject, in other words, out of the process, which, having made out most, handles it, in that relation, with the most consistent economy.[44]

James leaves the novelist his choice of a method that will best render the subject; therefore, the author gives to the novel a unity of tone and execution, and in so far as he selects incidents and episodes and does the necessary work of "going behind," he is part of the novel and orders its final structure. But to enter into the story and make the authorial self an integral part of the subject is unpardonable. Thus James's advice to Harriet Prescott is memorable: " 'Good heavens! Madam! . . . let the poor things speak for themselves!' "[45] Quite obviously he "insisted that the creator must regard his creation seriously, that he must respect its life with the strictest detachment and keep out all traces of his own irrelevant comments on his characters."[46] Consequently the method James admired was the method of Flaubert—one aptly described by Lubbock:

The *fact* of Emma is taken with entire seriousness, of course; she is there to be studied and explored, and no means of understanding her point of view will be neglected. But her value is another matter; as to that Flaubert never has an instant's illusion, he always knows her to be worthless.

He knows it without asserting it, needless to say; his valuation of her is only implied; it is in his tone—never in his words, which invariably respect her own estimate of herself.[47]

This type of rendering of a subject gave "what I hold most dear," wrote James, "a precious effect of perspective."[48] The dramatist is hardly a part of his drama in the way that a novelist like Thackeray, for instance, is a part of *Vanity Fair*. The "muffled majesty of irresponsible authorship"[49] is the furthest remove from the Jamesian concept of a dramatic novel. For James, the novelist's opinions, emotions, desires (like the dramatist's) have little connection with the opinions, emotions and desires of his characters. The novelist should seem merely to show what his characters do; he should create the illusion of life. So it is that James does not *tell* us what *he* sees in *What Maisie Knew;* he *shows* us what *Maisie* sees and thus the "design" of the story is "dignified by the most delightful difficulty, [which] would be to make and to keep her so limited consciousness the very field of my picture while at the same time guarding with care the integrity of the objects represented."[50] Nor, again, is the reader to be subjected to authorial opinion in *The Spoils of Poynton;* rather the spoils themselves will control values:

> The real centre, as I say, the citadel of interest, with the fight waged round it, would have been the felt beauty and value of the prize of battle, the things, always the splendid things, placed in middle light, figured and constituted, with each identity made vivid, each character discriminated, and their common consciousness of their great dramatic part established.[51]

The Awkward Age was, for James, the extreme in objectivity—a quality here to be achieved by his writing the novel in imitation of a play, "an example of the dramatic method pursued *à outrance*."[52]

The beauty of the conception was in this approximation

of the respective divisions of my form to successive Acts of a Play—as to which it was more than ever a case for charmed capitals. The divine distinction of a play—and greater than any other it easily succeeds in arriving at— was, I reasoned, in its special, its guarded objectivity.[53]
The Other House, too, was modelled on the drama and aspired to the objectivity of that form. Other novels that James also referred to as dramatized were ordered to objectivity either by some direct method—for instance, scene measuring scene as in *The Awkward Age*—or by some more elaborate one, as that of *The Turn of the Screw,* with its careful frame and shift in point of view.

The quality of objectivity, as James writes about it, derives from the consistency of treatment that the author applies to his subject. But that treatment is not haphazard. Rather it is a treatment that by its very nature forbids the author to *interfere* with the characters and their situation. The author, however, does not *interfere* when he structures his story in such a way as to distinguish clearly the intelligent from the stupid, the appearance from the reality, the ironic from the straightforward, and so forth, so long as he preserves the integrity of his treatment, which, *a priori,* must insist on showing rather than on the author's telling.

3. Economy

The very complexity implied in the quality of intensity exacted, for James, a representation at once rich with the reality of the situation and concentrated in its artistic form. The inherent difficulty in the interplay of complexity and concentration is the core of Jamesian economy. Economy for him is not mere brevity; if anything it is a "rich," "thick," "bristling" representation which balances the demands of matter and manner. A rich complex matter—most often related to an agent's fine consciousness—while inherently intense could lose its intensity if it were not represented: "the method is to be pushed as far as the subject can profit by it."[54] (Recall that "processes, periods, intervals, stages, degrees, connexions, may be easily enough stated . . . but it remains the very deuce to represent them. . . ."[55]) Yet if this representation were to get out of control, where would economy be? Where would beauty be?—for "in art economy is always beauty."[56] The problem of the artist is to create the work that has "drama enough, with economy."[57]

> To put all that is possible of one's idea into a form and compass that will contain and express it only by delicate adjustments and an exquisite chemistry, so that there will at the end be neither a drop of one's liquor left nor a hair's breadth of the rim of one's glass to spare—every artist will remember how often that sort of necessity has carried with it its particular inspiration.[58]

James faced this precise difficulty of economic representation, the need for "delicate adjustments," in his own playwriting career. When in the process of composing a stage version of *The Covering End,* he wrote Elizabeth Robins that "the real difficulty in the whole thing is *compression*—to play in an hour; for the action is already so close and tightly logical."[59] When he turned to the dramatic novel his problem was still one of economy.

> Any real act of representation is, I make out, a controlled and guarded acceptance, in fact a perfect economic mastery, of that conflict: the general sense of the experience, the explosive principle in one's material thoroughly noted, adroitly allowed to flush and colour and animate the disputed value, but with its other appetites and treacheries, its characteristic space-hunger and space-cunning, kept down.[60]

It is evident now that the constant and consistent emphasis which James placed upon the qualities of intensity, objectivity, and economy, with reference to novels and portions of novels which he designated as dramatized, logically categorizes these qualities as for him definitely dramatic; and his connection of these same qualities with the drama as such—especially that of Ibsen—supports such a classification. However, as was noted in the beginning, the drama achieved these qualities in a way not open to a narrative form. James's problem, therefore, was to develop within a narrative framework a structure that would approximate the qualities of a dramatic form.

B. ELEMENTS

The peculiar problem that James faced in dramatizing the novel was to create in a form controlled by a narrator and committed to action in the past—even if "the only interval between its occurring and the reader hearing about it is that occupied by the narrator's voice telling it"[61]—the qualities of intensity, objectivity, and economy peculiar to a dramatic form uncontrolled by a narrator and committed to action and dialogue in the present. In view of this hard reality Beach rightly asks: "But since, in the narrative, everything is really in the past, and nothing more present than anything else except by a trivial approximation in time, what is it gives us, in a story, the sense of the dramatic present?"[62]

The answer, perhaps, lies in the structure of the novel which James employed to incorporate the dramatic qualities and to convey an impression hardly distinct from that of the drama. The elements of this structure are (1) an imagistic, metaphoric, and symbolic matrix of language which becomes a means of presenting (2) an action that is structured in (3) scenes and (4) pictures and organized around (5) a centre that is often

14

intimately connected with the point of view in the novel. It would not be farfetched to look upon the action as the *subject* represented, the peculiar language matrix as the *means* of representing it, and the scenes, pictures and centres as the *manner* of representing the action.[63] Each of these elements of the structure of the dramatized novel means something quite special to Henry James. It will be well, then, carefully to consider each, starting with the means, moving to the subject and finishing with the manner. Once this is done, a clear idea of both the qualities and the elements of structure in James's dramatic novel will be available in the fullness of its theoretical meaning for application to his practice as a novelist.

1. Language

One of the principles of James's dramatized novel is that it should always represent. Such macrostructural devices as scenes and pictures, certainly, are integral elements *by which* this ideal is realized, but the minimal constant of the novel, its language, the medium *in which* the action is achieved, must also show, exhibit, and represent. Much attention has been given to the imagistic and complex metaphoric and symbolic qualities of James's use of language [64] (and somewhat less, too, to his structuring of it [65]). And in any consideration of the dramatic appeal that a novel makes, it is imperative to incorporate considerations of a like nature because they touch in many ways on each of the qualities of the novel, especially its presentational intensity.

The little tale "In the Cage" will serve to illustrate James's conscious manipulation of his medium. The *nouvelle* concerns a richly imaginative telegraphist, its heroine, who, because of income and social status, is in her view condemned to a rather humdrum existence. The present state of this existence is objectified by her job as a telegraphist; its future grayness is projected in her view of an impending marriage to the grocer Mr. Mudge. The heroine, intensely desirous of happiness, seeks a momentary and partial escape from reality in a half-imaginative "fling" with the romantic Captain Everard. She ironically serves her "romance" by being especially diligent in attending to the business of his telegrams, which serve his affair with Lady Bradeen. The girl is wonderfully happy in doing this for Everard, who himself has placed a tacit trust in her efficiency. The Platonic quality of their relation is endangered, nonetheless, after the pair meet for a park bench tête-à-tête, and he, on subsequent occasions, visits Cockers not so much to dispatch telegrams as to ogle the girl. The obviously romantic cast from which her imagination has struck him begins to chink somewhat, and the "betrothed of Mr. Mudge" finds the inside of the cage safer and less trying than its outside. The whole affair is resolved when she rescues Everard from a scrape and saves his romance with Lady Bradeen; the girl, now very much aware of reality, and exalting in the happiness of her little fling and her rescue of Everard, marches more peacefully and appreciatively to the arms of the waiting grocer.

This story of the developing awareness of the heroine is rendered quite vividly through the recurrent and incidental use of imagistic, metaphoric and symbolic language. The first paragraph serves as an instance.

It had occurred to her early that in her position—that of a young person spending, in framed and wired confinement, the life of a guinea-pig or a magpie—she should know a great many persons without their recognising the acquaintance. That made it an emotion the more lively —though singularly rare and always, even then, with opportunity still very much smothered—to see any one come in whom she knew outside, as she called it, any one who could add anything to the meanness of her function. Her function was to sit there with two young men—the other telegraphist and the counter-clerk; to mind the "sounder," which was always going, to dole out stamps and postal-orders, weigh letters, answer stupid questions, give difficult change and, more than anything else, count words as numberless as the sands of the sea, the words of the telegrams thrust, from morning to night, through the gap left in the high lattice, across the encumbered shelf that her forearm ached with rubbing. This transparent screen fenced out or in, according to the side of the narrow counter on which the human lot was cast, the duskiest corner of a shop pervaded not a little, in winter, by the poison of perpetual gas, and at all times by the presence of hams, cheese, dried fish, soap, varnish, paraffin and other solids and fluids that she came to know perfectly by their smells without consenting to know them by their names.[66]

Here we have an appeal to every sense in the most literal manner: "weigh letters, answer stupid questions, give difficult change" (visual and auditory); nearby was "the 'sounder' which was always going" (auditory); "her forearm ached with rubbing" (tactile and kinetic); there was an odor of perpetual gas (olfactory), and the taste of "hams, cheese, dried fish" (gustatory). The inhumanity of the girl's confined existence is given metaphoric detail: hers was a "framed and wired confinement, the life of a guinea-pig or a magpie." The monotony of her function is conveyed in a simile: she counted "words as numberless as the sands of the sea." And as one moves through the twenty-seven chapters of "In the Cage," the cage itself, which the reader is reminded of constantly, becomes a complex symbol of an inhuman existence at one time and of imaginative security at another.

In addition to what is represented by this initial passage, the story is shot through with other important sensuous details. The change which the girl doles out becomes a staple of the matrix as money becomes an all-important issue. Its abundance, its "golden" existence, contrasts with its "ha'penny" posture represented by the girl's reading and her fiancé's greasy (but neatly kept) account book. The water imagery introduced above spreads in "waves of fashion," to beauty on "a returning tide," and appointments "all swimming in a sea of . . . allusions"; ladies are found "swimming for their lives"; and throughout the tale the pages sound with the "plash of water." And these values are set in contrast with the less ingratiating sand: there is mention of "the small sanded floor of their contracted future" and a "desert of accepted derogation"; at one point the heroine visualizes Everard as "a tall lighthouse" while she herself, at another time, is merely "the sand on the floor." These series of connected images along with isolated ones (e.g., he "turned the knife in her tenderness"; "her private affairs rose and fell like a flame in the wind"; had she "no more feeling than a letter-box?") give to the "Cage" a perceptual texture and suggestiveness that a less imagistic prose might sacrifice. Even to the very detail of the names he bestows and withholds James is conscious of the impression he must make: the heroine telegraphist is too Protean to be boxed and tagged like her more commonplace grocer, "Mr. Mudge" (cf. *mud, smudge*). The enchanting Captain is "Everard" (either a pun on "ever odd" or an ironical use of the literal meaning: strong wild boar); and he is "nailed" by Lady "*Brad*een." The pretentious widow of a bishop appears with the surname "Jordan." It seems not at all strange that she cannot mix with the Lord named "Rye."

Wherever we touch it, it seems, James's language bristles, and it testifies to the fact that he did his "very deuce" to represent all the time.

2. *Action*

James distinguishes between dramatized novels and anecdotes by reference to the different subjects they treat. In the anecdote the character himself is the subject:

> The anecdote consists, ever, of something that has oddly happened to someone, and the first of its duties is to point directly to the person whom it so distinguishes. He may be you or I or any one else, but a condition of our interest—perhaps the principal one—is that the anecdote shall know him, shall accordingly speak of him, as its subject.[67]

The subject dramatized, however, does not relate to the question, "Of whom necessarily is it told?" Rather it finds expression in "a small straight *action*"[68] which places a novel "in that blest drama-light."[69] For "a complete and perfect little drama" the "little idea must resolve itself into a little action, and the little action into the essential drama aforesaid."[70]

Therefore, in those novels that he considered dramatized, James conceived his subject in terms of an action. Now the word *action* is an ambivalent one in the English language, and it remains so in Jamesian usage. At times it approximates the conception of action expressed by Aristotle's *praxis;*[71] here, for James, action is conceived as a pattern, as a whole, subsuming the variety of doing and experiencing in the novel. Thus James writes about his "long[ing] to represent an *action*";[72] he thinks about constructing "a little organic and effective Action";[73] he muses on the characters "in whom my 'rounded' action is embodied."[74] James thought of action in this sense as a unifying line in his dramatized novel; he therefore counseled the Duchess of Sutherland: "Take ... the *Ambassadors* very easily and gently: read five pages a day—be even as deliberate as that—but *don't break the thread*. The thread is really stretched quite scientifically tight."[75] When he con-

19

tinues this metaphor in a letter to Mrs. Everard Coates, it is obvious that he is referring to action: *"I* like a rope (the rope of *direction and march of the subject,* the action) pulled, like a taut cable between a steamer and a tug, from beginning to end."[76]

The march of the subject implies things that march, that happen; and it is precisely the phrase *things happening* (events, *pragmata*) that defines another meaning of the word *action.* In a November, 1894 note for *The Wings of the Dove,* after the query, "I get, at any rate, a distinct and rather dramatic action, don't I?" James traces a series of events which makes up the action of the novel.

> The poor girl has an immense shock. . . . She rallies. . . . She clings, she clings. . . . But the young man learns. . . . This enables him to measure. . . . He becomes ashamed . . . conceives a horror. . . . In that horror he draws close. . . . He tells. . . .[77]

James concludes his long note by considering how he would change the ending to suit a play: "The action would be the same up <to> the point of the girl's apparently impending death. . . ."[78] Clearly, by "action" he means here the individual events (the perceptions, thoughts, emotions, judgments, choices) which coalesce to form this more generalized action. Thus action is conceived not only generally as a whole but particularly as events that form that whole: "what will happen, who suffer, who not suffer, what turn be determined, what crisis created, what issue found. . . ."[79] To avoid confusion of terminology in subsequent discussion, action as a particular event will be referred to as *event,* and action as a whole will be referred to as *action.*

These two sides of action, the general and the particular— or, as James has it, the "tense cord" on which are strung "the

pearls of detail"[80]—form a complete action which is illustrative. Ruminating on the subject of *The Ambassadors,* he
writes: "The idea of the tale being the revolution that takes
place in the poor man by the particular experience, the incident in which this revolution and this impression embody
themselves, is the point *à trouver.*"[81] As this entry plainly
shows, an "idea" for James was not some sort of moral
aphorism. Rather "idea" for him is more aptly an "imaginative idea," which really remains incompletely expressed until
it is concretely embodied in a tale. The story "John Delavoy,"
for instance, was prompted by the stupidity of an editor (R. U.
Johnson) who rejected James's essay on Dumas because of the
discussion of sex in relation to the French theatre. When in
aggravation he pondered the germinal quality of this incident,
James searched for "some illustrative little action—little action illustrative of the whole loathsomely prurient and hum-
bugging business."[82] For "Paste" he had to "construct the illustrative action" that would reverse the situation in Maupas-
sant's "La Parure."[83] In each case James searched his mind to
"devise a little story, that will fit and express the phenomenon
I mean," and consequently he urged himself to the task:
"*Trouve donc, mon bon,* an ingenious and compact little action, which will bring this out."[84]

The whole notion of Jamesian action is evident in his remarks on "In the Cage." In that section of the preface to *What
Maisie Knew* devoted to this *novelle,* James notes that the
"action of the drama is simply the girl's 'subjective' adventure
—that of her quite definitely winged intelligence; just as the
catastrophe, just as the solution, depends on her winged
wit.[85] Here, while the wholeness of the action is evident in
James's seeing the story in terms of one action, he notes that
there are events which compose it—a catastrophe, a solution—

21

to say nothing of those that lead up to them. Also, this action is illustrative of the germinating idea of "In the Cage"—"the question of what it might 'mean,' wherever the admirable [telegraph] service was installed, for confined and cramped and yet considerably tutored young officials of either sex to be made so free, intellectually, of a range of experience otherwise closed to them."[86]

The action of "In the Cage" is symptomatic of the kind of action that is typically Jamesian—the "subjective adventure" of a "winged intelligence." In an 1885 letter to Violet Paget, which pointedly criticized her *Miss Brown,* James changed his tack toward its end and wrote:

> It's after my own heart in this sense: it is bravely and richly, and continuously psychological and that, for you, *life* seems to mean moral and intellectual and spiritual life, and not everlasting vulgar chapters of accidents, the dead rattle and rumble, which rise from the mere surface of things. I find the *donnée* of *Miss Brown* exceedingly in the right direction—a real subject, in the full sense of the word; carrying with it the revelation of character, which is the base of all things and finding its perspective in that; appealing too to the intelligence, the moral sense and experience of the reader.[87]

It is not surprising, then, that James at times refers to the consciousness as the stage on which his action takes place: it is "like a set and lighted scene, to hold the play."[88]

James was, indeed, the artist of "an 'exciting' inward life" which he believed to be "as 'interesting' as the surprise of a caravan or the identification of a pirate."[89] Quite logically, therefore, *The Spoils of Poynton* is not nearly so concerned with stolen bibelots and threatened litigations as it is with "a subject residing in somebody's excited and concentrated feeling about something. . . ."[90] Indeed, *What Maisie Knew* is so flushed with that " 'no end' of sensibility" imputed "to a slip of a girl"[91] that it makes the love games of grownups pale in its glow.

In view of such novels as these and in view of the recognized ethical and emotional introspection of the characters in all the works of the "major phase," the nature of the typical Jamesian action from *Poynton* onward is accurately recognized as one involving situations which trigger "a series of perceptions and choices involved with ethical problems of extraordinary complication"[92]—a type of action which, anything but flaccid, involves "the sharpest hazards to life and honour and the highest instant decisions and intrepidities of action."[93]

In summary, action is the subject represented in the dramatic novel. James conceives the action as a unifying whole in his novel; the whole action is composed of events, and it realizes some *donnée*. The nature of the action is frequently psychological in the sense that the development of states of consciousness provides mental and emotional events as significant as the extra-mental situations which either stimulate them or are stimulated by them. An action of the structure and the nature described is *a priori* more interesting than one less structurally rigid and psychologically relevant.

3. Scene

The function of the scene in a dramatic novel is to make perceptible, largely through dialogue and movement, both inward and outward aspects of an action taking place in a setting.[94] The outward aspect of the scene is clearly involved with movement, setting and gesture.[95] As Chapter XXIV of "In the Cage" ends, a conversation between the telegraphist and Mrs. Jordan is about to begin in the latter's rooms:

> The brown fog was in the hostess's little parlour, where it acted as a postponement of the question of there being,

besides, anything else than the teacups and a pewter pot and a very black little fire and a paraffin lamp without a shade. There was at any rate no sign of a flower; it was not for herself Mrs. Jordan gathered sweets (p. 490).

It is this dim little room with its dim little fire, its pewter pot and its teacups that the telegraphist prepares to leave:

Our young lady got up; recovering her muff and her gloves she smiled. . . .

Mrs. Jordan was now also on her feet. . . .

The girl considered, drawing on a glove. . . (p. 497).

Setting, movement, and gesture are clearly part of any scene. In the staged play they are visible to the spectator; in the novel they are often made visible through the voice of the narrator.

But no play, without resort to the soliloquy, was ever able to include an inwardness of the following kind in its properly constituted scene:

The mention of Lady Bradeen had frustrated for a while the convergence of our heroine's thoughts; but with this impression of her old friend's combined impatience and diffidence they began again to whirl around her, and continued it till one of them appeared to dart at her, out of the dance, as if with a sharp pick. It came to her with a lively shock, with a positive sting, that Mr. Drake was— could it be possible? With the idea she found herself afresh on the edge of laughter, of a sudden and strange perversity of mirth. Mr. Drake loomed, in a swift image, before her; such a figure as she had seen in open door-ways of houses in Cocker's quarter—majestic, middle-aged, erect, flanked on either side by a footman and taking the name of a visitor. Mr. Drake then verily *was* a person who opened the door! (p. 496).

An inwardness of this type, of a motion of realized thought, would require much dialogue for even a hint of total expression in a play. However, these sentiments are such by their nature that they could never be delicately expressed in a strained interpersonal colloquy. They are, in very fact, alien to the province of the playwright's scene. Their "inwardness is a kind of inwardness that doesn't become an outwardness—effectively—theatrically," as James once remarked.[96]

But obviously there is an inwardnesss for which the play is a conductor: there are certainties and opinions, pondered facts and possibilities that are expressible. This inwardness is given admirable expression in chapters XXV to XXVII of "In the Cage," where in this one scene (constituted by the three chapters and the barest fragment of XXIV) one is carefully and largely conversationally led from the heroine's discovery of Mrs. Jordan's impending marriage to Mr. Drake, the butler (and not Rye, the Lord), to the positing of motives for the impending marriage between Lady Bradeen and Captain Everard, to the prudent consideration on the heroine's part that her own marriage to Mr. Mudge must be, at the very latest, next month.

This inwardness and this outwardness with their samenesses and differences in reference to a play constitute aspects of the ordinary scenic unit in a James novel. And this inwardness and outwardness, which might properly be referred to as the subject of a scene, must be carefully structured. For a scene is not just conversation and gesture, thought and movement in a setting, but it is these things organically and logically related.

With reference to *Maisie,* "The Pupil," and "In the Cage," James wrote that they "demean themselves . . . as little constituted dramas . . . founded on the logic of 'scene'. . . ."[97] This logic finds explanation in the preface to *The Ambassadors,* where scenes are described as having a "logical start, logical turn, and logical finish."[98] The construction of the scene is such that it furthers action (from start, through turn, to finish) principally by conversation. Its formula is that of the play-wright's scene: "Action which is never dialogue and dialogue which is always action."[99]

The scene constituted by Chapters XXV to XXVII of "In the Cage" serves admirably to illustrate the formula of "dialogue which is always action" and the structure of start, turn, and finish. The conversation begins casually with the mention of Mrs. Jordan's affianced:

"I think you must have heard of Mr. Drake?" (p. 491). It progresses to the point where Mrs. Jordan reveals that Mr. Drake is going to leave Lord Rye and engage himself with Lady Bradeen.

"He's 'going,' you say, to her?"

At this Mrs. Jordan really faltered. "She has engaged him."

"Engaged him?"—our young woman was quite at sea.

"In the same capacity as Lord Rye."

"And was Lord Rye engaged?" (p. 495).

The girl's rumination of this puzzling matter leads to the realization that Mr. Drake *"was* a person who opened the door!" This point, at the end of Chapter XXV, constitutes the "logical turn." The girl, startled by the news of Mrs. Jordan's engagement to a butler rather than a Lord, gradually tempers her amusement with sympathy.

Her young friend stood there, still in some rigour, but taken much by surprise even if not yet fully moved to pity. "I don't put anything in any 'way,' and I'm glad you're suited. Only, you know, you did put to me so splendidly what, even for me, if I had listened to you, it might lead to."

Mrs. Jordan kept up a mild thin weak wail; then, drying her eyes, as feebly considered this reminder. "It has led to my not starving!" she faintly gasped (pp. 498f.).

The conversation next turns to Lady Bradeen, with whom Mr. Drake is to be connected, and passes from Mrs. Jordan's ensuing nuptials to those of Captain Everard and the Lady. The circumstances leading to the Everard-Bradeen match are discussed between the two until the incident relating to the salvaged telegram is reached (Mrs. Jordan's theory did not provide for the designation of the salvaged article).

"But what injury had he done her?"

"The one I've mentioned. He *must* marry her, you know."

"And didn't he want to?"

"Not before."

"Not before she recovered the telegram?"

Mrs. Jordan was pulled up a little. "Was it a telegram?"

The girl hesitated. "I thought you said so. I mean whatever it was."

"Yes, whatever it was, I don't think she saw *that*."

"So she just nailed him?" (p. 506).

The scene comes to a conclusion with the Captain and the Lady quite settled, and with the two women turning their attention to the proximity of their own marriages:

"She just nailed him." The departing friend was now at the bottom of the little flight of steps; and the other was at the top, with a certain thickness of fog. "And when am I to think of you in your little home?—next month?" asked the voice from the top.

"At the very latest." And when am I to think of you in yours?"

"Oh even sooner. I feel, after so much talk with you about it, as if I were already there!" Then "Good-bye!" came out of the fog (p. 506f.).

And these concluding words float from fog to fog and from scene to picture as the heroine exits into the London evening:

"Good-*bye!*" went into it. Our young lady went into it also, in the opposed quarter, and presently, after a few sightless turns, came out on the Paddington canal. Distinguishing vaguely what the low parapet enclosed she stopped close to it and stood a while very intently, but perhaps still sightlessly, looking down on it. A policeman, while she remained, strolled past her; then, going his way a little further and half lost in the atmosphere, paused and watched her. But she was quite unaware—she was full of her thoughts. They were too numerous to find a place just here, but two of the number may at least be mentioned. One of these was that, decidedly, her little home must be not for next month, but for next week; the other, which came indeed as she resumed her walk and went her way, was that it was strange such a matter should be at last settled for her by Mr. Drake (p. 507).

The scene has been written in a standard and characteristic[100] way with "each of the agents, true to its function, taking up the theme from the other very much as fiddles, in an orchestra, may take it up from the cornets and flutes or the wind instruments take it up from the violins."[101]

A scene of this kind treating the external and the internal logically, organically and, for the most part, in dialogue serves the dramatized novel in two principal ways: (1) it affords *complete* treatment to *all* the matter that the time of the scene encompasses; and (2) it provides for an interpersonal relationship which scene by scene gathers contrasting views of a situation; it provides, in short, for the "law of successive Aspects."[102]

In the scene between Mrs. Jordan and the heroine a complete discussion of matters takes place.[103] The reader is treated to Mrs. Jordan's acute consciousness of failure in her attempt to "nail" Lord Rye and in her need to survive with Mr. Drake.

He watches the disappointment and annoyance of James's heroine give place to pity and sympathy and the complete realization of the implications of Mrs. Jordan's position. The next incident is constituted by a brief battle of wits between the two women, each trying to learn something of the Everard-Bradeen situation while yet pretending to know almost everything. "It focuses rather upon the gradual comprehension of a situation than upon a series of new situations."[104] And finally, one overhears the inevitable projection of wedding dates and residence changes. This scene, then, like all scenes, is, in Lubbock's words, "expensive in the matter of time and space."[105] It is indeed a scene of the type that James described as standard: one "copious, comprehensive, and accordingly never short, but with its office as definite as that of the hammer on the gong of the clock, the office of expressing *all that is in* the hour."[106]

The scene in its admirable completeness also provides for the expression of the very last and most ironic of the varied aspects of "In the Cage"; for until this point in the tale the reader surmises that Mrs. Jordan is to be led to the altar on the arm of Lord Rye. In contrast with this supposed match and in contrast with the flirtation of the telegraphist with Everard, the nuptials of the girl and Mr. Mudge seem eminently second-rate. But poor Mrs. Jordan's present situation, and that coxcomb ordinariness which enables Lady Bradeen to "nail" Everard make Mr. Mudge appear a most suitable, if not illustrious, companion for the heroine.

The final scene brings into the situation what the girl had been loath to consider; but now, finally, "what our heroine saw and felt for in the whole business was the vivid reflexion of her own dreams and delusions and her own return to reality" (p. 499).

This discussion provides for the object, structure and function of the scene as a unit in itself and in relation to the whole novel. The scene is a structural unit composed mostly of dialogue. The structure of the dialogue is at times close to stichomythic. Through dialogue, gesture, and movement the scene comprehensively treats a portion of the novel severely limited by its brief duration in time. It serves either to make intelligible what has happened or to introduce some new element into the action. It develops through a logical movement that James described as start, turn and finish. As potentially objective discourse on a situation, it serves to provide one or more views of the meaning of events in the novel.

4. *Picture*

a. Picture as Structure

The meaning of the term *picture* is not easily pinpointed.[107] In different contexts it means different things, and the contexts themselves are so various that its meanings are manifold.[108] Perhaps the best approach to picture is through one, and to this end an early paragraph of "In the Cage" will serve:

> The barrier that divided the little post-and-telegraph office from the grocery was a frail structure of wood and wire; but the social, the professional separation was a gulf that fortune, by a stroke quite remarkable, had spared her the necessity of contributing at all publicly to bridge. Mr. Cocker's young men stepped over from behind the other counter to change a five-pound note—and Mr. Cocker's situation, with the cream of the "Court Guide" and the dearest furnished apartments, Simpkin's, Ladle's, Thrupp's, just around the corner, was so select that his place was quite pervaded by the crisp rustle of these emblems—she pushed out the sovereigns as if the applicants were no more to her than one of the momentary, the prac-

tically featureless, appearances in the great procession; and this perhaps all the more from the very fact of the connexion (only recognised outside indeed) to which she had lent herself with ridiculous inconsequence. She recognised the others the less because she had at last so unreservedly, so irredeemably, recognised Mr. Mudge. However that might be, she was a little ashamed of having to admit to herself that Mr. Mudge's removal to a higher sphere—to a more commanding position, that is, though to a much lower neighbourhood—would have been described still better as a luxury than as the mere simplification, the corrected awkwardness, that she contented herself with calling it. He had at any rate ceased to be all day long in her eyes, and this left something a little fresh for them to rest on of a Sunday. During the three months of his happy survival at Cocker's after her consent to their engagement she had often asked herself what it was marriage would be able to add to a familiarity that seemed already to have scraped the platter so clean. Opposite there, behind the counter of which his superior stature, his whiter apron, his more clustering curls and more present, too present, *h*'s had been for a couple of years the principal ornament, he had moved to and fro before her as on the small sanded floor of their contracted future. She was conscious now of the improvement of not having to take her present and her future at once. They were about as much as she could manage when taken separate (pp. 368f.).

This paragraph illustrates what for James is most typically meant by *picture* as a non-dialogue structure. Note that Cocker's, its people, and its provisions compose around the telegraphist in the sense that these are the things that she recognizes or that are there and possible for her to recognize. The inventory and the hurly-burly of the place are important only in their relation to the girl's sensibility. The inwardness of the picture is reflected in the girl's view of her situation: her detachment from the counter clerks because of her attachment to Mr. Mudge, her attitude toward his absence, her idea of marriage, her consciousness of her present and her future. And all indeed are presented in perceptually evocative prose. A picture, then, is never so much a description of an action or a situation as it is a description to which a value is attached because of the relation of the description to, or its meaning for, a character in the tale—in this case, the relation of Cocker's and the meaning of both it and Mr. Mudge for James's heroine. James referred to picture in this sense of the word as never "any literal record—anything merely narrative." In the words of Charles Crow, "We shall never find . . . much that is narration of entirely overt action; the action of someone's mind will be there too."[109] Characteristically, it is under the pressure of personal value that the fusion of time, place, incident and impression occurs. "I must picture it, summarize it, impressionize it, in a word—compress and confine it by making it the picture of what I see," James writes in the person of the narrator of "The Coxon Fund." [110] It is likely, then, that his most important use of the word *picture* as a non-scenic structure is this one of the rich, related, and summarized impression of an action or a situation.[111]

The function of the picture, in this sense, is fourfold: it is (1) to represent, (2) to summarize, (3) to provide for the personal sensibility; and (4) to prepare for scene.[112] James had little sympathy with novels that *told* and did not *show*, with novels which did not represent all the time. He complained when Robert Louis Stevenson failed to give even ever so brief a picture of a thoroughfare: "I utter a pleading moan when

32

you, e.g., transport your characters, toward the end, in a line or two from Leyden to Dunkirk without the glint of a hint of all the ambient picture of the 18th century road."[113]

To represent all the time is to allow the reader to "feel, taste, smell and enjoy"[114] what is happening, and to do this when there is no question of a scene must be to do it with a picture. After all, "One's poor word of honour" could not "pass muster for the show."[115] Bound by his own precept, James could not merely state that Mr. Mudge shone with an occasional redeeming flash of brilliance; he had to picture that flash through the girl's vision and impression of it.

> She felt that, oleaginous—too oleaginous—as he was, he was somehow comparatively primitive: she had once, during the portion of his time at Cocker's that had overlapped her own, seen him collar a drunken soldier, a big violent man who, having come in with a mate to get a postal-order cashed, had made a grab at the money before his friend could reach it and had so determined, among the hams and cheeses and the lodgers from Thrupp's, immediate and alarming reprisals, a scene of scandal and consternation. Mr. Buckton and the counter-clerk had crouched within the cage, but Mr. Mudge had, with a very quiet but very quick step round the counter, an air of masterful authority she shouldn't soon forget, triumphantly interposed in the scrimmage, parted the combatants and shaken the delinquent in his skin. She had been proud of him at that moment, and had felt that if their affair had not already been settled the neatness of his execution would have left her without resistance (p. 401).

Vivid remembrance of this little incident serves throughout the tale to remind the girl that Mr. Mudge has a potential and to remind the discriminating reader that Captain Everard, who does scarcely anything but send wires and smoke cigarettes, is not nearly so *gallant* (but infinitely more oleaginous).

This same passage is admirable in its economy as well as its dramatization. It is in fact a foreshortening—a picture severely summarized.[116] The girl, troubled by Mr. Mudge's theory that "their tastes were, blissfully, just the same," rescues herself from thorough annoyance through this flashback in which action is projected but condensed, time compressed and place sketched in. The foreshortening really functions as a bright little scene without a line of dialogue, and it is, in addition, shadowed with the value that the heroine places on its meaning. The impression of summary, the foreshortened effect, is in every way an important function of this picture. One notes simultaneously the character of Mr. Mudge and the sensibility of his fiancée as his actions are presented through her sense and valuation of them. It is significant, too, that this small section of Chapter IX of "In the Cage" is just a vignette in a montage which exhibits aspects of incidents and their meaning in the courtship of Mr. Mudge and the girl. It is a chapter and a picture which in its very representation prepares for Chapter X and the girl's conversation with the imposing grocer.[117] This final preparative one is perhaps the major function that James envisions for a picture. The picture is to set the stage in every needful way for the action of the scene. Thus, "the intervals between [scenes], the massing of the elements to a different effect and by a quite other law, remain, in this fashion, all preparative, just as the scenic occasions in themselves become, at a given moment, illustrative. . . ."[118] Everything that is not scene "is discriminated preparation, is the fusion and synthesis of picture."[119]

In recognition of his ordered variation in the use of scenes and pictures, James distinguished his practice as a system of alternation: "The great advantage for the total effect is that we feel, with the definite alternation, how the theme *is* being treated."[120] There are many points where scenes and pictures overlap, so that, as James noted, "each baffles insidiously the other's position."[121] Yet, while the picture shows action in which dialogue is reflected in snippets and the scene can record emotional states more usually awarded to pictorial treatment, it is evident that each structure more characteristically exerts its pressure in an area where the other is not so apt. The alternation of their appearance amounts to a system of structures which postures itself to accommodate the subject being developed: the typical scene treats in dialogue, interpersonally and objectively those thoughts and opinions, facts and probabilities that can find an outward expression; the picture typically treats those thoughts, emotions, and desires not easily expressed in conversation and also those actions and situations which press in upon and affect the consciousness. By means of scene and picture the novel treats the social and personal events of an action, the areas of conduct and consciousness.

b. Composition as Structure

James not only designated individual units in the structure of his novel by the term *picture,* but also, at times, referred to the whole novel as a picture. And to speak of that system of alternation which was just mentioned, is to touch on this second important meaning of *picture*—picture composed.[122]

The word *alternation* is the key to the whole question of the use of the scene and the picture in the novel. James thinks of the development of his novels as the alternation of parts that prepare for scenes and scenes themselves, both of which fuse to give the synthesis of picture. The dramatic scene in the novel is, then, a device used to frame the reader's attention; it focuses on one small area of the canvas; when all of these areas have been examined and put together, the picture emerges. The dramatic scene is thus a means to the end of developing the novel as picture.[123]

Once it is clear that to James a "picture without composition slights its most precious chance for beauty,"[124] it is evident why James was impatient with Walpole's *Maradick at Forty*.

... The whole is a monument to the abuse of voluminous dialogue, the absence of a plan of composition, alternation, distribution, structure, and other phases of presentation than dialogue—so that *line* (the only thing that I value in fiction etc.) is replaced by a vast formless featherbediness—billows in which one sinks and is lost.[125]

In his own productions from *Poynton* onward, James was quite conscious of the arrangement of lines and the placing of masses in his fictive pictures. In "In the Cage," for instance, the interview with Mrs. Jordan in Chapter II is balanced by the scene in Chapter XXVI. In Chapter II the girl feels inferior to Mrs. Jordan; by Chapter XXVI, the girl, engaged to her grocer, is superior to Mrs. Jordan, who has taken a butler in pursuit of a Lord. The girl's conversation with Mr. Mudge at Bournemouth as they sit on a bench overlooking the sea is calculated to balance her park bench conversation with Everard. Also, the main action of the story concerns the girl, Everard, and Mudge; the minor action involves Mrs. Jordan, Lord Rye, and Drake. Actually these are parallel and proportionate actions:

Girl : Everard :: Mrs. Jordan : Lord Rye

and

Girl : Mr. Mudge :: Mrs. Jordan : Drake

Parallelism is strikingly used in the last sentence of the tale, where the girl has the question of her future settled for her by the name of Drake. Indeed, the irony of the story is registered in the parallel and proportion, and it reaches its climactic resolution when both Mrs. Jordan and the heroine realize that everyday existence of the bread-and-butter kind is not viable in champagne dreams. "In the Cage," then, is quite carefully structured and in its parallels and proportions stands for James as a picture composed.

The word *picture*, thus, has a variety of meanings in James's usage. Two, however, are most important here. First, the picture is conceived as a basically non-dialogue structural block in the novel. It is an aspect of the manner of representation. It is usually related to and given value by the sensibility of a character. The picture can refer either to an interior state and event or to exterior ones in so far as they relate to a character's sensibility. The picture is used alternately with the scene, and in contrast with the scene, the picture is summarized and personal. Secondly, picture is used when the novel is conceived as balanced and composed. In this sense picture will be subsequently referred to as *picture composed* (while *picture* will always refer to the structural block which alternates with scene). The novel is viewed as a structure of carefully selected and proportioned events in an action.

5. Centre

A centre is at once an integral part of a novel and a means of organizing that novel.[126] Its use is governed by two principles of the novelist's art that James held sacred: one relates to the subject of the novel; the other, to its treatment, its composition.

The first is the notion that the only significant subject for a novel turns on someone's consciousness of some thing. This is generally suggested by James's own remarks, and particularly by a most significant one in which he professes that "I never see the *leading* interest in any human hazard but in a consciousness . . . subject to fine intensification and wide enlargement."[127] This governing conception of the Jamesian novel more than suggests that anything besides a developing felt relationship between a character and his situation is *a priori* an unsuitable subject for a novel.

The second principle governing the use of the centre relates to the notion of the novel as a picture composed. The novel must have causally and neatly related parts. In the Preface to *The Awkward Age* James explains the difficulty of giving symmetry to his proposed subjects and the necessity the novelist is under "to frame [them] in the square, the circle, the charming oval, that helps any arrangement of objects to become a picture."[128] Lubbock briefly elucidates the idea when he comments: "A novel is a picture, a portrait, and we do not forget that there is more in a portrait than the 'likeness.' Form, design, composition, are to be sought in a novel, as in any other work of art; a novel is the better for possessing them."[129] Since James refers to the novel as a picture composed, one may continue the metaphor and point to the organizing element of the picture—its centre.

> The "logical centre" or "commanding centre'" as a principle of composition in the novel corresponds to the establishment of a focal point in painting. It is, in painting, the ideal point where all lines converge, where the artist by his placing of figures and objects leads the eye to its inevitable resting point and the unity of the composition is realized. In the Jamesian novel the "commanding centre" is also a means to give unity to the structure of the work.[130]

The complications inevitably attendant on pursuing James from novel to novel revolve about the more and more complex use made of the centre. The best way to approach this problem is to introduce a dichotomy under the general notion of a centre as a means of organization. The centre may be simply conceived as (1) something which is a point of focus ("some place where all the rays meet or from which they issue"[131]), and/or as (2) something which focuses ("my preference . . . 'for seeing my story,' through . . . the sensibility of some . . . person who contributes . . . a certain amount of criticism and interpretation of it"[132]). The first may be referred to as a compositional centre; the second as a centre of vision. A final complication resides in the fusion of the two: there may be a centre of vision that is simultaneously the compositional centre of the novel.

Most of James's earlier novels illustrate the first type of centre—the centre that has a point of focus, a compositional centre. Theoretically, in *Roderick Hudson* all the events are significant only in so far as they affect the consciousnesss of Rowland Mallet. His consciousness is the compositional centre which orders the value and significance of every incident. The novel "remains in equilibrium by having found its centre, the point of command of all the rest. From this centre the subject has been treated, from this centre the interest has spread, and so, whatever else it may do or may not do, the thing has acknowledged a principle of composition and contrives to hang together."[133] Similarly Newman's consciousness is the compositional centre in *The American,* [134] just as Isabel Archer's is in *The Portrait of a Lady.*[135] Hyacinth Robinson functions in like manner for *The Princess Casamassima.*[136] In no sense, however, are any of these characters centres of vision throughout their respective novels—though frequently, of course, their sense of the action is projected. The centre of the action in *The Tragic Muse* is not a consciousness; rather it is a delicate young woman, Miriam Rooth, who stimulates the consciousness of Nick Dormer and Peter Sherringham.[137] *The*

Awkward Age finds its centre in a situation, Nanda's coming downstairs and into a circle of "free" conversation; all the incidents relate to this centre.[138]

Novels like *The Spoils of Poynton, What Maisie Knew* and *The Sacred Fount* have two centres—a compositional one and a centre of vision. But these on occasion tend to merge because the compositional centre is presented through the centre of vision's impression of it. Thus, for example, the spoils, the " 'things' themselves," organize the principal actions and reactions of Fleda, Mrs. Gereth, Owen, and Mona. But since at times Fleda is on the scene to project her view of the spoils, the value she gives them there tends to make her view of them the centre of composition.[139]

But the trick of the two-in-one is completely brought about by James in *The Ambassadors*. In this novel Strether's consciousness is both compositional centre and centre of vision. The only significance of the events in the story is the significance they have in developing Strether's sensibility, and the only way the events exist is through his impression of them.[140]

The Golden Bowl, like *The Wings of the Dove*, presents the final variation on centres. Here there are five centres of vision —The Prince, Charlotte, Fanny Assingham, Adam Verver, and Maggie—focusing on a compositional centre symbolized by the golden bowl.[141]

James's final development of the centre of consciousness, evident in his novels from *The Spoils of Poynton* to the fragmentary *Ivory Tower* and *Sense of the Past,* has brought about what a modern critic has called the effaced narrator.[142] It would be well to distinguish this narrator from the centre of consciousness, because thereby the important distinction between this centre and the point of view is made.[143] Perhaps the clearest distinction between the two is this: the point of view (the "relation in which the narrator stands to the story"[144]) is constant, whereas the centre of vision may change. For instance, in "In the Cage" the point of view is third person, external, and limited. The limiting factor is the consciousness of a character, i.e., a centre of vision. But since that character changes from the telegraphist to Mr. Mudge in one paragraph of Chapter X, the point of view remains the same (third person, external, limited) but the centre of vision changes (from the girl to her fiancé). The distinction is particularly useful in novels like *The Golden Bowl* and *The Wings of the Dove,* where the centres of vision are multiple, and in a novel like *What Maisie Knew,* where the centre of vision, Maisie's, requires the interpretation of the narrator. The point to realize, then, is that while the narrator's role is not emphasized, the narrator himself is never superfluous. And the effect that this has on objectivity is a matter which must be subsequently argued.

The structural function of centre of vision raises an area of meaning which has gained some prominence in the study of James—the problem of appearance and reality.[145] For purposes here, appearance refers to what a protagonist sees but does not understand, while reality refers to what is both understood and seen by him. In appearance there is a cleavage between seeing and understanding; in reality there is a fusion of the two. Appearance becomes reality in "In the Cage" when the girl realizes that she has been nursing an illusion about her relations with Everard and his society: ". . . What our heroine saw and felt for in the whole business was the vivid reflexion of her own dreams and delusions and her own return to reality. Reality . . . could only be ugliness and obscurity, could never be the escape, the rise" (p. 449). And this return, this fusion of appearance and reality, is precipitated by Mrs. Jordan's marriage to the butler rather than to the Lord: the thought "which came indeed as she resumed

41

her walk and went her way, was that it was strange such a matter should be at last settled for her by Mr. Drake" (p. 507).

Thus, a centre is one means of organizing a novel as an ordered composition. As such it admits a possible dichotomy into (1) a point of focus (compositional centre) and (2) something which focuses (centre of vision). These two can coalesce into one, as in *The Ambassadors*. The centre of vision also helps frame the events structured in scenes and pictures and allows an infusion of tension created through the manipulation of appearance (a cleavage between perception and meaning) and reality (a fusion of the two).

C. RELATIONS

With an understanding of the qualities and elements which for James form a dramatic novel, it seems reasonable to suppose that an hypothesis concerning the relations between them might be formulated. It seems obvious, for example, that the presentational intensity of the subject shown will be served by the highly perceptual matrix of language and the presentational immediacy of scenes and pictures. The composed aspect of intensity evident in its structural relations will be served by all the elements, but especially by the most organizing of them: the single action, the organizing centre, and the novel as picture composed. Intensity of a psychological nature should best be achieved by care in manipulating a centre of vision and the appearance and reality attendant upon it, as well as by picture as a structural unit emphasizing the personal impression of action and the ethical and emotional consciousness of a central character.

Objectivity will be best rendered by a centre of vision other than the author's. The law of aspects in an action will be served by the constant appearance of scenes (in rotation with

42

pictures) which present the views and clarifications of different characters concerning specific events.

And, finally, economy should be produced mainly through the offices of the single action controlled by an organizing centre—especially when it is a centre of vision. Also, of course, economy will be produced by pictures, and especially by those compressed pictures which are distinguished as foreshortenings. Through a single action, organized about a centre and partially presented through pictures, an action that bristles with representation will be viable.

The relationship between qualities and elements, it should be obvious, is such that while it is possible to find theoretical distinctions, it is impossible to manage practical separation. Indeed it seems that the more than hand-in-glove relationship between qualities and elements in the dramatic novel as James conceived it presses one to describe it in relation to both— to describe it as a novel achieving an intense, objective and economic representation in a narrative structure where the subject is an action structured in an imagistic, metaphoric, and symbolic matrix of language, presented through a pattern of alternating scenes and pictures, and organized about a centre or centres.

2

The Spoils of Poynton *and Intensity*

The simple attempt of some few characters to take possession of a country house filled with art treasures seems little likely to provide the central action in one of James's most intensely rendered novels. James, however, developed it into precisely that. He set in the midst of four characters a prize that for distinctly personal reasons would be as important to each of them as Helen of Troy was to the Greeks.[1] And he made these characters as different from one another as the opposing houses of Poynton and Waterbath. He set at odds Adela Gereth and her son Owen and placed in contrasting roles Fleda Vetch and Mona Brigstock. Each of these he distinguished from the others not only by a peculiar name[2] and distinctly personal traits of character, but also by an imagery which suggested the irreconcilable nature of the conflict among them. Thus he made the uncultured Mona's large patent leather pumps seem never to move in the same rarefied atmosphere in which the distinctly esthetic Fleda takes her flights,[3] and did not allow much common ground between an inept son, whose teeth seem to be his distinguishing mark,[4] and his mother, who characteristically compares her capabilities to those of Atlas.[5] By allowing the appeal of Poynton to affect this group, James set in motion somewhat more than a family squabble. The sharp differentia of character achieved on the level of names, traits, and imagery plausibly suggested a disagreement

44

of larger proportions. James, in fact, represented the struggle for the spoils as a small-scale internecine war. Since the conflict of the novel is realized in terms of this war, there seems no better way to begin a consideration of the dramatic quality of *The Spoils of Poynton* than with this matrix in which the conflict takes on a representational intensity through metaphor.

Almost mythical in its implications is Mrs. Gereth's statement which follows her move to Ricks with the spoils: " 'I've crossed the Rubicon, I've taken possession' " (p. 61). Fleda, startled at Adela Gereth's move, is consoled by her: " 'Oh, I know what you're thinking; but what does it matter when you're so loyally on my side?' It had come indeed to a question of 'sides,' Fleda thought, for the whole place was in battle array" (p. 72). When Owen consults with Fleda on the possibility of arbitration, his " 'I see you think she may refuse to discuss it at all' " receives the answer: " 'I'm only trying to be prepared for the worst. You must remember that to have to withdraw from the ground she has taken, to make a public surrender of what she had publicly appropriated, will go uncommonly hard with her pride' " (p. 96). It thus becomes impossible for Owen to "shut in Mrs. Gereth's face the open door of surrender: she would flare up and fight, flying the flag of a passionate, an heroic defense" (p. 166).

Very early in the novel Fleda is troubled with "the dread of inevitable surrender" of Poynton by Mrs. Gereth when Owen marries Mona (p. 15). Again Fleda speaks of surrender when she confronts Mrs. Gereth with the possibility: " 'I don't mean, naturally, that he should surrender everything . . .' " (p. 17). When, early in the novel, Owen fails to announce his engagement to Mona, "Mrs. Gereth's belief that their danger had dropped" is confirmed (p. 29). But later, in desperation, Adela Gereth speaks of giving up the house " 'if they'll let me take what I require!' " (p. 46). Owen comes to Poynton, at one point in the story, to check on his mother "in regard to the question of the perquisites with which she would retreat. The tension between them was now such that he had thus to reconnoitre without meeting the enemy" (p. 51). Having lost the war, Mrs. Gereth looks to future developments with apprehension: she awaits some further " 'stroke of diplomacy, some move in the game, some outwitting of *me*' " (pp. 241f.).

These few of many instances of the figurative language of battle[6] suggest how James defined and emphasized the conflict in *Poynton* by presenting it as a war. Through his consistent use of the war matrix the conflict achieves a degree of representational intensity. But James was not content to allow his novel this simple distinction. He realized in many of the events of the battle for the spoils a chance to achieve a structural intensity which would vitally enhance the dramatic quality of the novel. Thus there was effected in the overall picture of the action of *Poynton,* a symmetry of incidents. There is obviously an effect of balance in Mrs. Gereth and Owen, Mona and Fleda squared off around the centrally placed and hotly contested spoils. But there is an even more telling symmetry of incidents within this large square frame of the action as a whole. James has structured Poynton out of a series of events which complement one another. Event balances event, and the second event in each instance of a balanced pair of events is referred to the first in such a way that each acquires a new significance with reference to the other. The balancing consequently serves two purposes. It creates a pattern of structural symmetry in the novel, and it simultaneously adds a new dimension of meaning by creating cross-references through parallelism and contrast. Thus when early in the novel Owen meets Fleda in London, that event has its own meaning. When he meets her in London again, some chapters later, that event also has its own meaning.

But this pair of events also means something in the relation they bear to each other. Here two seemingly identical events, the meetings, come to mean something different when the relationship of the parties involved in them has altered through a change of circumstances. The first meeting is by accident; the second by design. The second meeting acquires a dimension that it could not have as an isolated event, and the contrast between each has as much meaning as the events do singly.[7]

In Chapter III Fleda comes to Poynton for the first time and she is overwhelmed by its beauty: " '*Now* do you know how I feel?' Mrs. Gereth asked when wondrous in the hall, three minutes after their arrival, her pretty associate dropped on a seat with a soft gasp and a roll of dilated eyes" (p. 21). This incident is balanced by Mona's arrival with her mother. The "rash innocence with which Mona had accepted the responsibility of observation" (p. 25) is noted. But since Mona does not verbalize her reaction, Mrs. Brigstock supplies the want. "Her mother, to make up for this, broke out universally, pronounced everything 'most striking' . . . but she jarred on Mrs. Gereth by her formula of admiration, which was that anything she looked at was 'in the style' of something else" (p. 27). Fleda's almost Dickensian swoon marks the degree of her appreciation in the same way that Mona's uninformed stoicism emphasizes the limits of her sensibility. But event balanced with event shows the reader what the girls are in relation to each other. James achieves here his ideal in representation: meaning is not asserted, but released by a juxtaposition of events.[8] A similar contrast exists between Chapter I, where Fleda and Mrs. Gereth react against Waterbath, and Chapter III, where Mona and Mrs. Brigstock fail to respond to Poynton.

The tone of future relations between the prospective mothers-in-law is set by means of another group of events. In Chapter III Mrs. Brigstock leaves a magazine with Mrs. Gereth:

. . . Poor Mrs. Brigstock, who at least was determined to rise and had brought with her a trophy of her journey, a "lady's magazine" purchased at the station, a horrible thing with patterns and antimacassars, which, as it was quite new, the first number, and seemed so clever, she kindly offered to leave for the house, was in the style of a vulgar old woman who wore silver jewelry and tried to pass off a gross avidity as a sense of the beautiful (p. 27).

Mrs. Gereth, however, "returns" the magazine in Chapter IV. Here she is speaking to Mona:

"For heaven's sake don't let your mother forget her precious publication, the female magazine with the what-do-you-call-'em—the greasecatchers. There!"

Mrs. Gereth, delivering herself from the doorstep, had tossed the periodical higher in air than was absolutely needful—tossed it toward the carriage the retreating party was about to enter. Mona, from the force of habit, the reflex action of the custom of sport, had popped out, with a little spring, a long arm and intercepted the missile as easily as she would have caused a tennis-ball to rebound from a racket. "Good catch!" Owen had cried, so genuinely pleased that practically no notice was taken of his mother's impressive remarks (p. 36).

The trips that Owen makes to Poynton and Ricks to negotiate with his mother clearly balance each other and serve to show the progress of the action. In Chapter IV he quarrels with his mother, but announces to Fleda his engagement to Mona. He also enlists Fleda to see his mother off the premises. Owen returns in Chapter V to tell his mother that she can take some "sticks" with her. Another trip, again in Chapter V, brings Owen to check on his mother's movements. In each case Owen does the same thing—he comes to Poynton—but each visit is for a different reason and in the face of slightly altered circumstances. Consequently the decline in family relations can be traced through this series of visits representing parallel actions that become most meaningful in contrast with each other.

Fleda's arrival at Poynton, described above, balances and contrasts with her arrival at Ricks in Chapter V. " 'Why it's charming!' she exclaimed a few hours later, turning back again into the small prim parlour from a friendly advance to the single plate of the window" (p. 53). But this reaction hardly equals Fleda's breathless collapse on her first seeing Poynton. Rather it is the second visit to Ricks which parallels that first introduction to Poynton and contrasts with the above: Fleda "had been perfectly prepared to be surprised at Ricks, for Mrs. Gereth was a wonder-working wizard . . . but the impression in wait for her on the threshold made her catch her breath and falter" (p. 70). And this arrival is finally paralleled by her arrival at the dispoiled but transformed Ricks in Chapter XXI: "Her arrival took the form of a surprise very nearly as violent as that of the other time. The elements were different, but the effect, like the other, arrested her on the threshold: she stood there stupefied and delighted at the magic of a passion of which such a picture represented the low-water mark" (p. 247).

The conversation of Fleda and Owen in Chapter VIII balances that of Fleda and Mrs. Gereth in Chapter X. Here contrast is arrived at through minute parallelisms. In VIII Owen admits to Fleda that his marriage is delayed; in X Fleda denies that she has any knowledge of a delay in the marriage. In VIII it is clear to the reader that Fleda loves Owen; in X she tells Mrs. Gereth that she "hates" him. In VIII Owen says that Mona will break off the engagement; in X Fleda tells Mrs.

Gereth that Mona will never break it off. In VIII Fleda tells the truth on all matters; in X she lies about the important ones. Here, obviously, Chapter X means very little without Chapter VIII, but in contrast with it, reveals a great deal about Fleda's devotion to Owen's honor.

Besides these many incidents mentioned, there are a number of others that could also be cited as elements in the balanced structure of *Poynton*. There is the Ricks with the maiden aunt exterminated (p. 79), and the Ricks with the maiden aunt revived (p. 248); there are two occasions when Fleda shuts the door in Owen's face (pp. 99, 103); both Mona and Fleda examine their shoes (pp. 28, 113), and Mona's are large (p. 29) whereas Fleda's are small (p. 133); Mrs. Gereth's collection of *objets d'art* contrasts with Mr. Vetch's collection of match boxes and gimcracks. These and others are instances which form a complex system of balances within the large symmetrically structured action of *Poynton*. These balanced events are not gratuitous trappings, but parts of a rigid structure which by contrast and parallelism makes the events of the novel more meaningful. *The Spoils of Poynton* emerges from an analysis of this kind as a most carefully structured novel which in both large and small demonstrates a high degree of structural intensity.

The psychological intensity of *Poynton* stems from the difficulties attendant upon attempts to get the spoils. As James indicated from the first, the battle over the "Things" would set in motion intellectual, emotional and volitional responses in those who contested each other for them.[9]

Mrs. Gereth thinks that Poynton should be hers, and she is terrified at the prospect of forfeiting it to Mona. She decides to appropriate it until time eliminates the prospect of loss. Throughout the novel she is engaged in speculations over strategic maneuvers. She has continuously to make crucial decisions. And the tension under which she leads her life—because of the ever present prospect of what she might lose—is very great.

Her son Owen, though not nearly so intelligent as she, also has his moments of tension. He decides to marry Mona. Subsequently, however, he comes to doubt the wisdom of his decision and the reality of his love when Mona demands Poynton as a prerequisite to marriage. The kindness of Fleda further complicates Owen's life and redirects his emotions. His passion, at least temporarily, becomes connected with Fleda. He finds himself emotionally racked by the opposite pull of honorable commitments to Mona and a desire for freedom to love Fleda. Consequently the conflict over Poynton becomes a severe trial for him.

Both Owen's and his mother's involvements in the action are usually presented in scenes—but scenes which always include Fleda. They are presented, too, indirectly, through Fleda's view of them. Fleda's involvement, however, is presented directly in pictures and in scenes. Her thoughts and emotions are projected in pictures, and the difficulty she experiences in concealing the true nature of her affections is presented in scenes with Mrs. Gereth and Owen. Throughout the novel the reader sees the increasing pressure that the girl must withstand. Since she has most to gain (in Owen and Poynton), she also has most to lose by a decision which would jeopardize her future. Yet this is precisely the decision that climaxes her coming to grips with the moral-psychological problem in the novel.

The problem develops because of the complex set of circumstances in *Poynton* and because of the obligations Fleda contracts with those involved in strained relationships. Owen is engaged to Mona. He has not only contracted himself to the girl, he has also contracted his inheritance, Poynton and its spoils. Legally, Owen inherited Poynton on the death of his father, and Adela Gereth had no voice in its disposition. Unable of his slow self to bring his mother to relinquish Poynton, Owen seeks the aid of Fleda: "The special business she herself thus became aware of being charged with was that of seeing Mrs. Gereth safely and singly off the premises" (p. 44). Fleda, however, is supposedly Adela Gereth's tried and true friend. She is engaged to aid Mrs. Gereth, not Owen.

The peculiar form of aid that Mrs. Gereth hopes to obtain from Fleda is her marrying Owen. Mrs. Gereth would be only too happy to part with the treasures of Poynton if Fleda were to be their custodian. The situation becomes further complicated when Fleda falls in love with Owen. Fleda, loving Owen and contracted to his mother, now finds it in her power to snatch Owen from Mona and possess the spoils as a proxy for Mrs. Gereth. However, she cannot do this without dulling her peculiar sense of justice, because Owen is engaged to Mona and has promised to marry her. In Fleda's socio-ethical view of the situation, if Owen does not keep his promise, he will "break faith" and consequently lose "honor." The engagement promise is looked upon as something supremely serious, and Owen, too, comes to take this view of it.

Now Fleda's course of conduct is not an easy one for her to follow. She loves Owen; he has expressed his love for her as well. Besides, she feels the tie of friendship contracted with Adela Gereth. Nevertheless, "to be right," "to keep faith," "to preserve honor," and "to be just to Mona"—that is, to adhere unfailingly to what for her are principles of honorable human behavior—she cannot marry Owen.[10]

This complex set of circumstances would in its own right imply a degree of psychological intensity. But James has raised the intensity to a peak by his careful manipulation of techniques of presentation. All that has already been noted should serve to indicate that there is nothing of the "splendid waste" that James felt characteristic of many novels. There is scarcely a wasted word, much less a wasted character, event, name, or image. The central feud over the spoils of Poynton by characters who are defined by their actions in relation to Poynton (which stands as a positive value) is part of James's technique. The use of recurring images in relation to character presentation is part of James's technique. Motivations, names, and imagery unmistakably realize the characters. These characters are thrown into conflict over Poynton, and the conflict is described in a vocabulary of war so as to be intensified. Again, this is part of James's technique. None of these things is superfluous; each contributes to the total effect of the novel. Together they solidify in an unmistakable fashion the central moral and psychological problem in *Poynton*. And this problem is made even more acute and vivid by James's presentation of it through a centre of vision—Fleda Vetch—that controls the function of appearance and reality in the novel.

The primary concern of the reader of *The Spoils of Poynton* is not what will happen to the spoils: they are not interesting for their own sake, but they acquire interest because their use or abuse will ultimately help to determine the degree of Fleda's excellence. Understandably James insisted that "somehow . . . character . . . would unmistakably be the key to my modest drama, and would indeed alone make a drama of any sort possible. . . ."[11] The most important part of this novel is Fleda, "the free spirit, always much tormented and by no means always triumphant," who is "heroic, ironic, pathetic or whatever, and . . . 'successful,' only through having remained free."[12]

Consequently James intended to make *Poynton* interesting, not primarily through the disposition of the spoils, but through Fleda's character, which is so largely determined by her attempt to direct the disposition of them. And to focus interest on Fleda, James used her as the centre of vision in his novel. The reader is permitted to see and to feel with Fleda, and he is denied any other source of knowledge. Into this highly sensitive centre of vision filter all the complexities of the situation; here they are disentangled and judged.

Unlike *The Portrait of a Lady*, in which Isabel Archer passes from innocence to knowledge by having appearances dispelled so that she may come to recognize the reality of her situation, or again, unlike *What Maisie Knew*, in which the ultimate happiness of the little girl depends upon her fusing of appearances and meanings, or unlike so many other Jamesian fictions wherein appearance and reality must converge for the protagonist thoroughly to understand his position in a situation, *The Spoils of Poynton* has a heroine who is always in complete possession of the reality behind the appearance. James intensifies his psychological dimension by allowing Fleda as centre of vision to manipulate appearances in the service of her cause. What she does, oddly enough, to preserve her integrity is keep the reality of her and their situations hidden from Owen and his mother. To prevent Mrs. Gereth from forcing her hand, Fleda hides the fact of her love for Owen, his overtures to her, and Mona's threat to break off her engagement if Poynton is denied her. To have Owen act honorably, Fleda refuses to acknowledge her love for him. The climaxes in the novel are reached when Fleda can no longer prevent appearance and reality from converging in the minds of Owen and his mother. When Owen visits her at Maggie's, Fleda breaks down and admits her love. When Mrs. Gereth learns from Mrs. Brigstock that Mona's engagement is virtually off, she makes the mistake of returning the spoils to Poynton in the belief that Owen will now marry Fleda. However, she guesses wrongly, and ironically precipitates the action which causes her to lose all. The climactic scene between Fleda and Mrs. Gereth in Chapter XVIII follows this mistake. By this point in the novel the falsity of appearance has been cleared away sufficiently for the reality to be revealed. Fleda no longer has need to manipulate appearances; according to her peculiar ethical standards, she has preserved her integrity, helped Owen to act honorably, and caused a moral sense to glimmer in Adela Gereth.[13] Thus James concentrates attention on Fleda, and with her juggling of appearances and realities he keeps his reader in a state of suspense, pressing him to the point where he fears that Fleda will drop some hitherto delicately handled fact and consequently ruin her adept and intriguing performance.

The intensity of *Poynton* is more complex than this discussion has served to indicate: it is obvious that whereas imagery is part of representational intensity, it is also part of the structural intensity as well. Also, whereas balanced events are elements of structural intensity, it is equally clear that each of these is part of the representational intensity in so far as it impresses one as something seen rather than as something told. And although the centre of vision is integral to the novel's psychological intensity, it also serves structural intensity to the degree that it provides a consistent view of the varied relations in the action. This discussion, then, is one of emphasis. What this emphasis stresses is that language, scene, and picture are the most important means for representational intensity; that symmetry (or picture composed) and the use of a compositional centre are the most significant features of structural intensity; and that centre of vision and appearance-and-reality are the chief components of the novel's psychological intensity.

While it remains true that *The Spoils of Poynton* leaves one with the final impression of its intensity, it is not without economy and objectivity. Economy is fostered by the centre of vision, the language, and the careful balance of events. In each case there is an instance of representation with a double function. Through the centre of vision the reader is given both the event and Fleda's reaction to it. The care in selecting a word which is not only a name, but one that characterizes, and the care in selecting not only an image, but one that symbolizes predominant character traits, clearly works toward economic representation. The fact that an event frequently balances a previous event makes it meaningful without the need of further comment. *The Spoils of Poynton* is quite economic.

The objectivity in *Poynton* is effected through its centre of vision. The view of the action is not James's; it is Fleda's. Although he is the narrator, James records not his observations, but Fleda's. James does slip sometimes and become, as John Tilford called him, the "Old Intruder,"[14] but the slips are rare (pp. 5, 10, 38, 108) and of the kind that make the reader aware of a narrator, but not of the pressure of his opinions.

In conclusion, then, *The Spoils of Poynton* is a novel with all the qualities that for James were dramatic: it is intense, economic, and objective. It arrives at these qualities through a careful handling of certain elements: of an action in language structured in scenes and pictures and presented through a centre. For James, then, in every sense, *Poynton* was a dramatic novel.

3

What Maisie Knew *and Economy*

Simply stated, *What Maisie Knew* is the story of a little girl's life from her sixth to her twelfth year. It details the process of her growing up in an atmosphere of irresponsibility and squalid sexual promiscuity, and it marks stages of her development ranging from the most unconscious naïveté to a satisfying intellectual and emotional maturity. James, in writing this novel, arranges a group of sophisticated elders around a young girl who is as fresh as they are wilted. His innocent heroine is given over to a world of initiates who push and pull her from house to house and from country to country in abortive efforts to dispose of her in some way or another, and who come to realize, to their shame, that no one but she is responsible enough to decide what her future must be. James places the girl with a mother and father who care less about her than do her stepmother and stepfather, who, in their turn, are less interested in their charge than is her governess, Mrs. Wix. He places the child initially with parents who use her as a brickbat which they periodically hurl at one another, and then with the father's present wife and mother's present husband, who find the child a suitable mask to hide their adultery. And finally James awards the girl to a somewhat silly but selfless old woman who has no interest but the child's and who alone can give her a stability that neither parents nor stepparents can provide. *What Maisie Knew* is then a novel about a topsy-turvy world: it details innocence where there should be taint, selfishness where there should be love, irresponsibility where there should be responsibility, and maturity where there should be immaturity. As such *Maisie* stands as one of James's most sustained pieces of irony, which in the process of becoming such reveals itself as one of his most economically developed novels.

The most important choice that James had to make for his novel was a centre of vision. The choice was of major importance because by it he had to reconcile his desire to write an "ugly little comedy"[1] with his determination to hold as the focus of the novel the "very principle of Maisie's appeal, her undestroyed freshness."[2] There arose for him the "acute constructional question, the endless expressional question"[3] of centre of vision. Through whose vision could James most satisfactorily project to a little girl, who was its pariah, the forbidden world of the sexual foible?[4] The answer was as ironic as the novel itself. Only the little girl could be an adequate reflector of the sordid world in which she lived. Only a child sensitive enough to see yet young enough to misunderstand was adequate for the venture. To exploit the cleavage between a child's seeing and its understanding would be the single salutary way to realize meanings which must otherwise be lost: to have the girl see and not understand was precisely to have the reader both see and understand.[5]

> To that then I settled—to the question of giving it *all*, the whole situation surrounding her, but of giving it only through the occasions and connections of her proximity and her attention; only as it might pass before her and appeal to her, as it might touch her and affect her, for better or worse, for perceptive gain or perceptive loss: so that we fellow witnesses, we not more invited but more expert critics, should feel in strong possession of it. . . .[6]

In her presence Maisie's lack of understanding provides her elders a latitude that would be positively impossible—because positively impracticable—in the presence of anyone who could grasp the meaning of a compromising situation or a *double-entendre*. With Maisie as centre of vision, however, James realized one possible means of eating his cake and having it too. He got all the squalor that his "ugly little comedy" required and all the innocence that gave Maisie her appeal, and in the interplay between the ugly and the innocent the novel's world of values took shape.

What, indeed, could be more ugly, innocent or comic than Maisie's periodic rides in a coach? Having lived the first six months after the divorce of her parents with her father, Maisie prepares to join Ida Farange, who awaits her in her carriage. Beale Farange, however, detains the child long enough to have her con a message of greeting—which shocks her nurse and amuses his friend—for her mother:

The supreme hour was to furnish her with a vivid reminiscence, that of a strange outbreak in the drawing-room on the part of Moddle, who, in reply to something her father had just said, cried aloud: "You ought to be perfectly ashamed of yourself—you ought to blush, sir, for the way you go on!" The carriage, with her mother in it, was at the door; a gentleman who was there, who was always there, laughed out very loud; her father, who had her in his arms, said to Moddle: "My dear woman, I'll settle *you* presently!"—after which he repeated, showing his teeth more than ever at Maisie while he hugged her, the words for which her nurse had taken him up. Maisie was not at the moment so fully conscious of them as of the wonder of Moddle's sudden disrespect and crimson face; but she was able to produce them in the course of five minutes when, in the carriage, her mother, all kisses,

ribbons, eyes, arms, strange sounds and sweet smells, said
to her: "And did your beastly papa, my precious angel,
send any message to your own loving mamma?" Then it
was that she found the words spoken by her beastly papa
to be, after all, in her little bewildered ears, from which,
at her mother's appeal, they passed, in her clear shrill
voice, straight to her little innocent lips. "He said I was
to tell you, from him," she faithfully reported, "that
you're a nasty horrid pig!"[7]

This exchange serves as an instance of the general atmosphere
—of the mother's regard for the father and the father's for
the mother—to which Maisie's innocence is blissfully exposed
before the ladies at Ida's and the gentlemen at Beale's.

Another carriage ride introduces Maisie to an intime relationship between her father and her governess. For Maisie
the words and the actions mean one thing; to the reader they
mean another. Maisie is going from Ida's to Beale's with her
father and Miss Overmore, whom she has left six months pre-
viously:

"Did papa like you just the same while I was gone?" she
enquired—full of the sense of how markedly his favour
had been established in her presence. She had bethought
herself that this favour might, like her presence and as if
depending on it, be only intermittent and for the season.
Papa, on whose knee she sat, burst into one of those loud
laughs of his that, however prepared she was, seemed always, like some trick in a frightening game, to leap forth
and make her jump. Before Miss Overmore could speak
he replied: "Why, you little donkey, when you're away
what have I left to do but just to love her?" Miss Overmore hereupon immediately took her from him, and they
had a merry little scrimmage over her of which Maisie

caught the surprised perception in the white stare of an old lady who passed in a victoria. Then her beautiful friend remarked to her very gravely: "I shall make him understand that if he ever again says anything as horrid as that to you I shall carry you straight off and we'll go and live somewhere together and be good quiet little girls." The child couldn't quite make out why her father's speech had been horrid, since it only expressed that appreciation which their companion herself had of old described as "immense." To enter more into the truth of the matter she appealed to him again directly, asked if in all those months Miss Overmore hadn't been with him just as she had been before and just as she would be now. "Of course she has, old girl—where else could the poor dear be?" cried Beale Farange, to the still greater scandal of their companion, who protested that unless he straight-way "took back" his nasty wicked fib it would be, this time, not only him she would leave, but his child too and his house and his tiresome troubles—all the impossible things he had succeeded in putting on her. Beale, under this frolic menace, took nothing back at all; he was indeed apparently on the point of repeating his extravagance, but Miss Overmore instructed her little charge that she was not to listen to his bad jokes: she was to understand that a lady couldn't stay with a gentleman that way without some awfully proper reason.

Maisie looked from one of her companions to the other; his was the freshest gayest start she had yet enjoyed, but she had a shy fear of not exactly believing them. "Well, what reason *is* proper?" she thoughtfully demanded.

"Oh a long-legged stick of a tomboy: there's none as good as that." Her father enjoyed both her drollery and his own and tried again to get possession of her—an effort deprecated by their comrade and leading again to something of a public scuffle (pp. 31f.).

Situations of a like kind occur throughout the novel. Ida, though married, brings Mr. Perriam to visit Maisie in her schoolroom. Maisie and Sir Claude (Ida's second husband) meet Ida and the Captain in Kensington Gardens. Sir Claude arranges a meeting with Beale's wife (formerly Miss Overmore) in Earle's Court. Mrs. Beale and Maisie meet Beale and the Countess at the Exhibition there. Maisie has an interview with her father and the Countess, his mistress, in the latter's apartments. Each of these situations dramatizes for the reader the progressive disintegration of parents and stepparents. Each, likewise, while immediately beyond Maisie's total comprehension, is posited as a fact that her subsequent maturity demands she eventually understand:

> By the time she had grown sharper, as the gentlemen who had criticised her calves used to say, she found in her mind a collection of images and echoes to which meanings were attachable—images and echoes kept for her in the childish dusk, the dim closet, the high drawers, like games she wasn't yet big enough to play (p. 12).

> It was literally a moral revolution and accomplished in the depths of her nature. The stiff dolls on the dusky shelves began to move their arms and legs; old forms and phrases began to have a sense that frightened her (p. 14).

This process of attaching meanings to "images and echoes" of her earlier life represents the continuous movement of Maisie's mind toward the fusion of the thing seen and its meaning—it represents the process of her maturation.

The cleavage between appearance and reality in Maisie's

vision of events provides not only for her innocence amid her elders' guilt, but also for the essential amusement of those scenes in which Mrs. Wix attempts to "bring out" Maisie's "moral sense"—attempts to make squalor appear squalid to Maisie's eyes. Mrs. Beale (second wife of Maisie's papa) and Sir Claude (second husband of Maisie's mamma) are in love and want to live together as husband and wife. Each proclaims that he is "free" because Beale has "bolted" with the Countess and Ida with Mr. Tischbein. Mrs. Wix and Maisie examine the possibility of Mrs. Beale's and Sir Claude's being Maisie's guardians while Mrs. Wix is retained as her governess:

Maisie took her up before she could further phrase Mrs. Beale's capability. "Stay on as *my* companion—yes. Stay on as just what you were at mamma's. Mrs. Beale *would* let you!" the child said.

Mrs. Wix had by this time fairly sprung to her arms. "And who, I'd like to know, would let Mrs. Beale? Do you mean, little unfortunate, that *you* would?"

"Why not, if now she's free?"

"Free? Are you imitating *him?* Well, if Sir Claude's old enough to know better, upon my word I think it's right to treat you as if you also were. You'll have to, at any rate —to know better—if that's the line you're proposing to take." Mrs. Wix had never been so harsh; but on the other hand Maisie could guess that she herself had never appeared so wanton. What was underlying, however, rather overawed than angered her; she felt she could still insist —not for contradiction, but for ultimate calm. Her wantonness meanwhile continued to work upon her friend, who caught again, on the rebound, the sound of deepest provocation. "Free, free, free? If she's as free as *you* are, my dear, she's free enough, to be sure!"

"As I am?"—Maisie, after reflexion and despite whatever of portentous this seemed to convey, risked a critical
echo.

"Well," said Mrs. Wix, "nobody, you know, is free to
commit a crime."

"A crime!" The word had come out in a way that made
the child sound it again.

"You'd commit as great a one as their own—and so
should I—if we were to condone their immorality by our
presence."

Maisie waited a little; this seemed so fiercely conclusive. "Why is it immorality?" she nevertheless presently
enquired.

Her companion now turned upon her with a reproach
softer because it was somehow deeper. "You're too un-
speakable! Do you know what we're talking about?"

In the interest of ultimate calm Maisie felt that she
must be above all clear. "Certainly; about their taking
advantage of their freedom" (pp. 271f.).

Not long after this exchange Maisie realizes the importance of
the situation. It seems not so much that she comes to grasp the
sexual implications of Ida's escapades with Mr. Perriam, Lord
Eric, the Captain, and Mr. Tischbein or of Beale's with his
varied retinue or even of Mrs. Beale's and Sir Claude's wanting to live together: it is not then so much Maisie's getting
her "moral sense" (as Mrs. Wix understands it) as it is her
getting a moral sense far and away more human—"something
still deeper than a moral sense" (p. 354). Maisie realizes that
for all their brilliance her stepparents (and *a fortiori* her parents) are not really human because they are not really free,
whereas her governess for all her comparative dinginess is human precisely because she is free.[8] Yet Maisie is not so narrow-
minded as Mrs. Wix. The governess represents for the girl an

especial aspect of humanity in her freedom, but so too does Sir Claude in his humaneness. But Sir Claude is trapped and afraid; he is a man made weak by his attachments. Maisie, so much like her beloved Sir Claude in her human goodness and her utter consideration, refuses to compromise the freedom in which these virtues must operate by placing herself in a situation which can only be debilitating. She refuses not to be free. Thus Maisie finally chooses to live with Mrs. Wix because with her she can be most free and consequently most truly human. Maisie has come clearly to see Sir Claude's fear in his inability to give up Mrs. Beale and take her to Paris:

> She had had a real fright but had fallen back to earth. The odd thing was that in her fall her fear too had been dashed down and broken. It was gone. She looked round at last, from where she paused, at Sir Claude's and then saw that his wasn't (p. 345).

Mrs. Wix, concentrating on the narrowly moral only, and not on the radically human as well, emphasizes the "moral sense" in a limited way.[9] It is no wonder that while she sees Maisie as finally achieving a "moral sense," she cannot realize the proportions of it. The novel ends simply on that note: "She still had room for wonder at what Maisie knew."[10]

It seems then quite definite that James's choice of Maisie as centre of vision was a sound one. It enabled him to explore in the world of his novel the values inherent in the innocence, comedy, and squalor which attend the child's view of her situation. With this centre of vision James found an excellent technique for exploring the essential ironies of his novel.

The process of Maisie's gradually developing awareness of the implications of her situation occupies some six years. It is difficult to think of many James novels that cover so long a span of time. Even those novels devoted to an action which occupies considerably less time more than double *Maisie's* size.

It is a paradox of sorts, then, that this novel, which James considered to be so economically written, should be so spread over Maisie's young life. Yet a span of years was essential to the ironic effect and had to be manipulated in such a way as to enhance it. James managed to highlight his ironies by correlating the passing of time with changing residences, changing attitudes, and changing faces.

Maisie is six years old when Beale and Ida Farange are divorced. She spends the first six months after the separation at her father's, where Moddle is her nurse. It is there that her phantasmagoric existence takes shape with her father's tossing her mother's letters "bang into the fire," with her lighting of cigarettes for gentlemen who pinch her, with trips to Kensington Gardens in Moddle's company, with mamma calling papa "beastly," and papa calling mamma a "nasty horrid pig."

The persistence of similar features in Maisie's young life makes them constants for "a couple of years" (p. 14). And with this phrase steeped in the particulars that precede, James gives his reader the sense of time passing while saving the space of making it pass. He, in effect, sets Maisie in a carriage with Ida on one page (p. 13) and two pages later, because of the impressions gleaned from the six months with Beale, he returns the reader to a Maisie who is plausibly "a couple of years" older and seemingly just stepping from the carriage for another half-year with Ida.[11] Papa's Moddle gives place to mamma's Miss Overmore and Beale's pinching gentlemen to Ida's squealing ladies as Maisie's naïveté is supplanted by a new system of practiced stupidity:

> She puzzled out with imperfect signs, but with a prodigious spirit, that she had been a centre of hatred and a messenger of insult, and that everything was bad because she had been employed to make it so. Her parted lips locked themselves with the determination to be employed

no longer. She would forget everything, she would repeat nothing, and when, as a tribute to the successful application of her system, she began to be called a little idiot, she tasted a pleasure new and keen. When therefore, as she grew older, her parents in turn announced before her that she had grown shockingly dull, it was not from any real contraction of her little stream of life. She spoiled their fun, but she practically added to her own (p. 15).

Maisie returns to Beale's, and to papa she brings Miss Overmore, who deserts Ida for the child. Back at her mother's six months later, Maisie meets her new governess in the person of Mrs. Wix. By Chapter V, when she returns to Beale's, Maisie has lived through the dreadful routine for at least three years. Yet the reader is treated to only three removes, but they are so highlighted by two memorable carriage rides, three governesses, retinues of smoking gentlemen and laughing ladies, Maisie's naïveté and practiced stupidity, and the shameless coarseness of her parents that they speak eloquently for three years and more. By this time, however, each of the parents is disgusted with Maisie because she no longer serves each as an adequate cudgel with which to beat the other. Rather, the little girl has become a financial burden only, one which each parent is happy to doff and transfer to the other. And Ida is the first to take advantage of her period of independence by leaving Maisie for an extended period with Beale—some "weeks and weeks" longer than the agreed six months.

Beale is rescued from the onerous duty by Ida's second husband, Sir Claude, who whisks the child to Ida's for a period equal to her stay at her father's. By the end of this stay with her mother, her stepfather has formed an alliance with her father's second wife. Thus Sir Claude takes Maisie to Mrs. Beale, her stepmother, for "several weeks" (p. 137). Awakening scruples lead him, however, to remove the child from the center of an adulterous relation to the more peripheral Boulogne, where Maisie is reunited with Mrs. Wix. Some few days later the novel ends. By this time Maisie is almost twelve years old, having aged six years, not in the smooth passing of slow time, but in the endless bustle of changed residences, new governesses, new mammas and new papas, and new gentlemen for the old mamma and new ladies for the old papa, and new insights into the whole of her experience. The sharply etched series of ironic events and all that they suggest and imply become figures on a clock—not of hours, but of months and years.

As might be expected in a James novel which encompasses six years in some three hundred and fifty pages, these and other important events need to be economically represented.[12] One way that James achieves economy is by presenting one event which suggests one or many other preceding events that the reader has not witnessed. Consequently a scene like the one in which Maisie rides in the carriage with Beale and Miss Overmore serves at least two purposes. It shows the present and reflects the past. Six months have elapsed since Maisie left Miss Overmore, then her governess at Beale's. Now, the reader knows, Miss Overmore is more than Maisie's governess; she is also Beale's mistress. The present suggests the past, and while the event detailing the present is given, the past incidents leading up to it are there by suggestion.

James is also fond of using a moment of revelation to summarize action in a significant manner. Toward the novel's end, when Sir Claude arrives in Boulogne to join Mrs. Beale, Maisie and Mrs. Wix, he tells his little charge that he hasn't seen Mrs. Beale since his arrival.[13] Maisie and Sir Claude then prepare to leave for breakfast:

> "We'll go to a cafe." Maisie was already at the door; he glanced round the room. "A moment—my stick." But there appeared to be no stick. "No matter; I left it—oh!"

He remembered with an odd drop and came out.

"You left it in London?" she asked as they went downstairs.

"Yes—in London: fancy! (p. 321f.).

It does not take a great deal of imagination to realize that Sir Claude left the stick in Mrs. Beale's room and that he has once again lied to Maisie. With the stick, so with the carriage ride: the present suggests the unspoken past.

When Maisie and Sir Claude meet Ida and the Captain in Kensington Gardens, James writes a scene that shows a great deal of economy. Before Sir Claude and Maisie discover the identity of Ida's male companion, they speculate on his identity.

"Then who is it with her?"

"Blest if I know!" said Sir Claude.

"Is it Mr. Perriam?"

"Oh dear no—Perriam's smashed."

"Smashed?"

"Exposed—in the City. But there are quantities of others!" Sir Claude smiled.

Maisie appeared to count them; she studied the gentleman's back. "Then is this Lord Eric?"

For a moment her companion made no answer, and when she turned her eyes again to him he was looking at her, she thought, rather queerly. "What do you know about Lord Eric?"

She tried innocently to be odd in return. "Oh I know more than you think! Is it Lord Eric?" she repeated.

"It may be. Blest if I care!"

. . . .

"Is it—*is* it Lord Eric?"

Sir Claude smoked composedly enough. "I think it's the Count" (pp. 140f., 142).

Next, Maisie and Sir Claude meet Ida. As she leaves to chat with the Captain, Maisie hears Sir Claude's initial salvo " 'You damned old *b* . . .!'—she couldn't quite hear all. It was enough, it was too much: she fled before it, rushing even to a stranger for the shock of such a change of tone" (p. 145). Maisie then settles down with the Captain while Sir Claude and Ida argue. The reader is treated to a foreground of peace and reassurance while in the background the fury of marital hate is unleashed just out of earshot.

The Captain speaks with Maisie and tells her how fine a woman her mother is. To the Captain Ida is "good"; indeed, she is an "angel." His quieting effect on Maisie is profound. His conversation with her is so extraordinarily contrary to all that is known about Ida that one gets a new insight into her character: in love, she is a Jekyll; out of love, a Hyde. All of Ida's charms come to a head in the Captain's view of her.

Yet while in the foreground the reader sees Maisie enthralled by the blue-eyed, straw-complexioned soldier holding her hand, he never loses sight of the figures in the background. Although nothing but Sir Claude's first shot is heard, the battle is fierce, to be sure. From it Sir Claude returns flushed and out of temper and in eloquent silence testifies to its cruelty.

The Kensington Gardens scene, then, is quite economical with its foreground and background actions and with the multiple events suggested by that single catalogue of Ida's lovers which Maisie so assiduously reviews with Sir Claude and the Captain. Yet there is more to the scene than this double exposure of past and present. It serves as a center of reference for other scenes in the novel and by so doing contributes by its very economy to an ironic effect. The irony of the Kensington Gardens scene finds its complete development in the complementary function of the two other major events in the novel. With Maisie's interview with Ida at Folkestone and her meeting with Beale at the Countess's, the Kensington Gardens scene forms a vignette in that whole picture which the novel carefully composes. It is, in fact, in the framework of the novel as picture composed that the balanced sequence of events—partially represented by the Kensington scene—makes its full ironic effect felt.

If Beale can decide that Maisie's life will be spoiled by her living with Ida, Ida can as easily discern Beale's corrupting influence on her daughter. For the "child's good" each keeps Maisie from the other for six months every year (p. 4). But this bruited altruism is balanced by a quiet selfishness when each parent sees that the child is no longer interested in being told the defects of the other (p. 19). The desire to possess Maisie is turned into a scheme to be free of her. When Beale pursues his flirtation with Miss Overmore, it seems only fitting that Ida should have "picked up" someone on the Continent (p. 31). If Ida can take a second husband in Sir Claude, Beale can take a second wife in Miss Overmore. If Maisie can bring together Beale and Miss Overmore in a guilty love affair, she can just as easily take Mrs. Beale from her husband and introduce her to Sir Claude. If Maisie, while walking with mamma's husband, can meet her mamma with the Captain in Kensington Gardens, she can also, while walking with her papa's wife, meet her papa and the Countess at the Exhibition. And if mamma and papa can be unfaithful in marriage to their second spouses, the second spouses can be faithful outside of marriage to each other. Thus vice for vice and lover for lover Ida and Beale are equals. And James can pick no more economic way of dramatizing this than by showing the two doing such similar things.

Not only do events like these parallel each other, but also they serve to show the ever observant Maisie that the world of "saying" and that of "doing" are two different worlds as far as mamma and papa are concerned. Ida's walk in Kensington Gardens not only parallels Beale's at the Exhibition, but also gives Maisie an opportunity to hear her mother praised in a way that denies all she has learned and is yet to learn about her. When the Captain says to Maisie, " 'Look here, she's true!' " the child is so charmed by the man with the eyes like pale flowers that she mistakes his statement for fact. Maisie is much wiser, though, after her talk with Ida at Folkestone, where she asks her mother when she is going to South Africa with the Captain:

"The Captain? What Captain?"

"Why when we met you in the Gardens—the one who took me to sit with him. That was exactly what *he* said."

Ida let it come on so far as to appear for an instant to pick up a lost thread. "What on earth did he say?"

Maisie faltered supremely, but supremely she brought it out. "What you say, mamma—that you're so good."

"What 'I' say?" Ida slowly rose, keeping her eyes on her child, and the hand that had busied itself in her purse conformed at her side and amid the folds of her dress to a certain stiffening of the arm. "I say you're a precious idiot, and I won't have you put words into my mouth!" This was much more peremptory than a mere contradiction. Maisie could only feel on the spot that everything had broken short off and that their communication had abruptly ceased. That was presently proved. "What business have you to speak to me of him?"

Her daughter turned scarlet. "I thought you liked him."

"Him!—the biggest cad in London!" Her ladyship towered again, and in the gathering dusk the whites of her eyes were huge.

Maisie's own, however, could by this time pretty well

match them; and she had at least now, with the first flare of anger that had ever yet lighted her face for a foe, the sense of looking up quite as hard as any one could look down. "Well, he was kind about you then; he *was*, and it made me like him. He said things—they were beautiful, they were, they were!" . . . "I've thought of him often since, and I hoped it was with him—with him—!" Here, in her emotion, it failed her, the breath of her filial hope.

But Ida got it out of her. "You hoped, you little horror—?"

"That it was he who's at Dover, that it was he who's to take you. I mean to South Africa," Maisie added with another drop. . . ." "You're a dreadful dismal deplorable little thing," Ida murmured. And with this she turned back and rustled away over the lawn (pp. 223-225).

The Kensington Gardens tête-à-tête with the Captain serves as a point of reference for this latter Folkestone interview. It also parallels Maisie's meeting with her father and the Countess at the fair. But in the subsequent exchanges between Maisie and Beale and Maisie and the Countess in the latter's apartments, the Captain's kindness is contrasted with her father's selfishness, and the Countess's liberality with her mother's stinginess. There is scarcely anything as charming in the novel as the Captain's offer to have Maisie come with him and Ida (p. 153f.), or anything as low as Beale's attempt (throughout Chapter XIX) to leave Maisie behind as he beats a retreat down a path of lies. The same charm and sordidness are set in contrast again as Maisie leaves the Countess "with her hand full of coin" (p. 196) and her mother with disappointed and empty hands (p. 225). Also, Beale's attempt to free himself from his duties toward Maisie parallels Ida's attempt to do the same at Folkestone. Beale tells his daughter that he is going to America and Ida feigns a trip to South Africa. But the

Countess shows Beale to be a liar by inviting Maisie to join them at Spa (p. 194), just as Mrs. Wix shows Ida to be a liar by announcing her presence in London with Mr. Tischbein (p. 247). The scene at Kensington reaches to Folkestone and both Kensington and Folkestone look to the Countess's apartment. The comparisons and contrasts set up among these scenes pursue to its ultimate point the irony of the selfishness of parents and the liberality of strangers, the absence of love where it should be and the presence of it where it need have no claim. Here, by means of parallel events, three scenes complement and extend meanings beyond their immediate contexts; here, in his pursuit of economy, James has flushed the novel's most telling irony.

James comes to grips in *Maisie* with the problem of representation by compression. Here his notable technique is to telescope time in a series of foreshortened incidents which cover the first half of the novel. When he resorts to more elaborate scenes in its second half, they are so interrelated that their very comprehensiveness—in reaching into the past and anticipating the future—is economic. In addition to this use of the foreshortened picture and the expanded scene James capitalizes on a centre of vision. Through Maisie the reader is constantly referred to the actual situation and her reaction to it, while clearly preserving an awareness of what a proper response should be.[14]

It is a paradox, in a way, that the centre of vision, the use of scene and picture, and the structural neatness of balanced events should be the very things from which the intensity and objectivity of the novel arise. But it is quite evident that Maisie's view of the situation gives the reader both Maisie and the situation and consequently a psychological intensity. Also, the use of parallel events that form part of the novel's structural intensity eliminates the need of the narrator's commenting on the situation. Just as the Countess shows Beale to be a liar, and Mrs. Wix shows Ida to be one, and Sir Claude's stick points to his failure in truth, so too there are many additional events in the novel which measure others past and/or to come. Again, then, in *What Maisie Knew,* James *shows;* he does not *tell.*[15]

There seems indeed to be no better comment on *Maisie*'s economy than the fact that it does so much with so little. And there seems to be no better comment on *Maisie* as a dramatic novel, in James's sense of the term, than that the "so much" represents the dramatic qualities of economy, intensity, and objectivity, and "so little" represents the technique of James's dramatic novel—an action cast in scenes and pictures and presented through a centre of vision.

4

The Awkward Age *and Objectivity*

In *The Spoils of Poynton* and *What Maisie Knew* James attempted to create a dramatic effect, at least in part, through a symmetry of events. In *The Awkward Age* he tried to repeat his success on a grand scale. He described his plan for the novel in relation to a design that he sketched for the publishers of *Harper's Weekly*:

> I remember that in sketching my project for the conductors of the periodical I have named I drew on a sheet of paper . . . the neat figure of a circle consisting of a number of small rounds disposed at equal distance about a central object. The central object was my situation, my subject in itself, to which the thing would owe its title, and the small rounds represented so many distinct lamps, as I liked to call them, the function of each of which would be to light with all due intensity one of its aspects.[1]

Each of the "lamps" was to be "completely a scenic thing,"[2] "dialogue organic and dramatic,"[3] which would give the novel "the divine distinction of the act of the play . . . its guarded objectivity."[4] What James tried to do in *The Awkward Age* was create through a series of dialogues a novel which, while possessing the attributes of a play, could be spatially contemplated as a pictorial design.[5] The conception was so unusual and the undertaking so complex that complete success was

76

almost impossible. It is, in fact, easy enough to discern areas of failure. James made the triple mistake of employing a rigorous symmetry that was not organic to his material, of substituting the trappings of dialogue for the essence of drama, and of sacrificing, in dull prolixity, intensity and economy to objectivity.

There is, certainly, no arguing the fact that James's series of dialogues achieves great objectivity. Take, for instance, those snatches of conversation which Mrs. "Brook" has with her son, the Duchess, and her husband concerning Harold's going to Brander. In Chapter IV Mrs. Brooks encounters her son Harold just after he has taken five pounds and some sovereigns from her secretary:

"One can't live anywhere for nothing—it's all bosh that a fellow saves by staying with people. I don't know how it is for a lady, but a man's practically let in—"

"Do you know you kill me, Harold?" Mrs. Brookenham woefully interposed. But it was with the same remote melancholy that she asked in the next breath: "It wasn't an *invitation*—to Brander?"

"It's as I told you. She said she'd write, fixing a time; but she never did write."

"But if *you* wrote—"

"It comes to the same thing? *Does* it?—that's the question. If on my note she didn't write—that's what I mean. Should one simply take it that one's wanted? I like to have these things *from* you, mother. I do, I believe, everything you say; but to feel safe and right I must just *have* them. Any one *would* want me, eh?"

Mrs. Brookenham had opened her eyes, but she still attached them to the cornice. "If she hadn't wanted you she'd have written to keep you off. In a great house like that there's always room."

The young man watched her a moment. "How you *do* like to tuck us in and then sit up yourself! What do you want to do, anyway? What *are* you up to, mummy?"

She rose at this, turning her eyes about the room as if from the extremity of martyrdom or the wistfulness of some deep thought. Yet when she spoke it was with a different expression, an expression that would have served for an observer as a marked illustration of that disconnectedness of her parts which frequently was laughable even to the degree of contributing to her social success. "You've spent then more than four pounds in five days. It was on Friday I gave them to you. What in the world do you suppose is going to become of me?"

Harold continued to look at her as if the question demanded some answer really helpful. "Do we live beyond our means?"

She now moved her gaze to the floor. "Will you *please* get away?"

"Anything to assist you. Only, if I *should* find I'm not wanted—?"

She met his look after an instant, and the wan loveliness and vagueness of her own had never been greater. "Be wanted, and you won't find it. You're odious, but you're not a fool."[6]

This sounds like a wholly different affair when the Duchess broaches it with Mrs. Brook:

"Where's he off to?" this friend enquired with a casual advance and a look not so much at her hostess as at the cushions just rearranged.

"Oh to some places. To Brander to-day."

. . . .

"Who's to be at Brander?" she asked.

78

"I haven't the least idea—he didn't tell me. But they've always a lot of people."

"Oh I know—extraordinary mixtures. Has he been there before?"

Mrs. Brookenham thought. "Oh yes—if I remember—more than once. In fact her note—which he showed me, but which only mentioned 'some friends'—was a sort of appeal on the ground of something or other that had happened the last time."

The Duchess dealt with it. "She writes the most extraordinary notes."

"Well, this was nice, I thought," Mrs. Brookenham said —"from a woman of her age and her immense position to so young a man."

Again the Duchess reflected. "My dear, she's not an American and she's not on the stage. Aren't those what you call positions in this country? And she's also not a hundred."

"Yes, but Harold's a mere baby."

"Then he doesn't seem to want for nurses!" the Duchess replied. She smiled at her hostess. "Your children are like their mother—they're eternally young."

"Well, *I'm* not a hundred!" moaned Mrs. Brookenham as if she wished with dim perversity she were. "Every one's at any rate awfully kind to Harold." She waited a moment to give her visitor the chance to pronounce that eminently natural, but no pronouncement came—nothing but the footman who had answered her ring and of whom she ordered tea (pp. 48-50).

When Edward asks about his son, he gets half of what Harold got and half of what the Duchess got from his wife; he gets, in short, a mixture of the true and the false:

"And where's Harold?" he went on.

"He's at Brander. That is he will be by dinner. He has just gone."

"And how does he get there?"

"Why by the South-Western. They'll send to meet him."

Brookenham appeared for a moment to view this statement in the dry light of experience. "They'll only send if there are others too."

"Of course then there'll be others—lots. The more the better for Harold."

This young man's father was silent a little. "Perhaps—if they don't play high."

"Ah," said his mother, "however Harold plays he has a way of winning."

"He has a way too of being a hopeless ass. What I meant was how he comes there at all," Edward explained.

"Why as any one comes—by being invited. She wrote to him—weeks ago."

Brookenham just traceably took this in, but to what profit was not calculable. "To Harold? Very good-natured." He had another short reflexion, after which he continued: "If they don't send he'll be in for five miles in a fly—and the man will see that he gets his money."

"They *will* send—after her note."

"Did it say so?"

Her melancholy eyes seemed, from afar, to run over the page. "I don't remember—but it was so cordial" (pp. 69f.)

These conversations admirably characterize Mrs. Brook as an unscrupulous opportunist and equivocator. The narrator does not say that she is one; nobody, in fact, ever says so. But the reader sees what happens from scene to scene and judges for himself. James, in casting the burden of decision upon the reader, makes his novel most objective. But one must ask whether all the talk required to create the objectivity is worth the space and time it occupies. Mrs. Brook equivocates and seizes opportunities throughout the novel. And Harold is really a very minor character who does enough other odious things—ranging from speaking vulgarly to stealing and committing adultery—to obviate the need of the pages devoted to his Brander excursion. Besides, this discussion is so peripheral to the central problem focusing on Nanda that it is almost irrelevant. James overburdened the reader, then; what could have been left out or foreshortened he needlessly expanded for the sake of dialogue and symmetry.

It is true that James achieved objectivity by his method, but where do the other dramatic qualities of intensity and economy fit into this system? They seem, indeed, on occasion, to be the victims of it. On two, three, or more occasions the reader hears in the interest of objectivity different people talk at length about the same thing. He is thus presented with different views of an event. But the appositeness of the event itself to the central situation does not appear to have been considered. The seemingly irrelevant is as fully treated as the seemingly relevant. This disproportion is glaringly illustrated by the tangential love affairs of Cashmore and Carrie Donner, Captain Dent-Douglas and Fanny Cashmore receiving as full a treatment in Chapter XIII as does the central climactic scene of the novel in Chapter XXX. Subordination of treatment fails to go hand in hand with subordination of meaning. There is consequently the danger of generating what is not a truly proportioned dramatic effect; moreover, the incidents inspiring the conversations are seldom coterminous with them, so that what results is conversation about one's feeling about something past or to come. Speech does not run parallel with and flash from event, but it circles an absent midpoint with the dim glow of hypotactic dialogue.

In Chapter XX, for instance, Longdon offers to endow Nanda if Van will marry her. He and Van discuss this point at length and then pass on to Mitchy's chances of winning Nanda's hand, Mrs. Brook's inevitable opposition to Longdon's plan, and Nanda's extraordinary knowledge. In Chapter XXI Van goes over Longdon's offer at length with Mrs. Brook. Also, they discuss Mitchy's chances. Mrs. Brook then registers her opposition to the Longdon plan. In Chapter XXII Mitchy arrives. With Mrs. Brook and Van he discusses Longdon's offer and much of the same ground is covered. Mrs. Brook again registers her opposition and Mitchy's chances are again discussed. It is true that in Chapter XX there is only Longdon and Van, in Chapter XXI Mrs. Brook and Van, and in Chapter XXII Mrs. Brook and Van and Mitchy. But by this time the issue is suffocating. However, it is not left to die just yet. Chapter XXVI parallels Chapter XX. Here Van talks with Mitchy at Mr. Longdon's, whereas in Chapter XX Van talked with Mr. Longdon at Mitchy's. The conversation is about Longdon's offer, Mitchy's marrying Aggie (which will end his chance for Nanda), and Nanda's knowledge. It is obvious that the continual use of the same themes with a slight variation is characteristic of the structure of *The Awkward Age*. No one can deny that through it the ground is thoroughly covered, but no one can aver that the same topics (which relate to the past and the future) have not been forced again and again into lengthy discussions (in the present) by a method which *a priori* refuses to recognize the value of subordination and synthesis.

In addition, there is inherent in this tendency toward ubiquitous meticulosity the danger of another type of reduplication. For instance, James describes a character in the manner of the enlightened observer of the scene and then allows that character to speak in such a way as to testify to the truth of the description. Thus, Edward Brookenham:

When Mr. Brookenham appeared his wife was prompt. "She's coming back for Lord Petherton."

"Oh!" he simply said.

"There's something between them."

"Oh!" he merely repeated. And it would have taken many such sounds on his part to represent a spirit of response discernible to any one but his mate.

"There have been things before," she went on, "but I haven't felt sure. Don't you know how one has sometimes a flash?"

It couldn't be said of Edward Brookenham, who seemed to bend for sitting down more hinges than most men, that he looked as if he knew either this or anything else. He had a pale cold face, marked and made regular, made even in a manner handsome, by a hardness of line in which, oddly, there was no significance, no accent. Clean-shaven, slightly bald, with unlighted grey eyes and a mouth that gave the impression of now working easily, he suggested a stippled drawing by an inferior master. ... He had never in his life answered such a question as his wife had just put him and which she would not have put had she feared a reply. So dry and decent and even distinguished did he look, as if he had positively been created to meet a propriety and match some other piece, that lady, with her famous perceptions, would no more have appealed to him seriously on a general proposition than she would, for such a response, have rung the drawing-room bell (pp. 66f.).

Mrs. Brook continues her conversation with her husband, taking up the subjects of the Duchess and Petherton and Nanda and Tishy, of which Edward knows nothing—thus his many "Oh's"—and she knows everything. As described, Edward Brookenham is somewhat inane. In conversation he is no less so. There seems to be little reason for both description and conversation; add to this the fact that there will be more information on the Duchess and Petherton later and that the reader already knows all about Tishy and Nanda, and there is even less reason for the scene. In fact, Chapter VI, for the most part, is expendable.[7]

One can, finally, mention the fact that some conversations are so tenuous and drawn out as to contribute little to the novel and much to wearing down the reader's patience. Here, for instance, Mrs. Brook talks with Nanda about Longdon:

"Was it at the place he took you to that he gave you tea?" she then went on.

"Yes, at the Museum. We had an orgy in the refreshment-room. But he took me afterwards to Tishy's, where we had another.

"He went *in* with you?" Mrs. Brook had suddenly flashed with eagerness.

"Oh yes—I made him."

"He didn't want to?"

"On the contrary—very much. But he doesn't do everything he wants," said Nanda.

Mrs. Brook seemed to wonder. "You mean you've also to want it?"

"Oh no—*that* isn't enough. What I suppose I mean," Nanda continued, "is that he doesn't do anything he doesn't want. But he does quite enough," she added.

"And who then was at Tishy's?"

"Oh poor old Tish herself, naturally, and Carrie Donner."

"And no one else?"

The girl just waited. "Yes, Mr. Cashmore came in."

Her mother gave a groan of impatience. "Ah *again?*"

Nanda thought an instant. "How do you mean, 'again'? He just lives there as much as he ever did, and Tishy can't prevent him."

"I was thinking of Mr. Longdon—of *their* meeting. When he met him there that time he liked it so little. Did he like it any more to-day?" Mrs. Brook quavered.

"Oh no, he hated it."

"But hadn't he—if he should go in—known he *would?*"

"Yes, perfectly. But he wanted to see."

"To see—?" Mrs. Brook just threw out.

"Well, where I go so much. And he knew I wished it."

"I don't quite see why," Mrs. Brook mildly observed. And then as her daughter said nothing to help her: "At any rate he did loathe it?"

Nanda, for a reply, simply after an instant put a question. "Well, how can he understand?"

"You mean, like me, why you do go there so much? How can he indeed?"

"I don't mean that," the girl returned—"it's just that he understands perfectly, because he saw them all, in such an extraordinary way—well, what can I ever call it?— clutch me and cling to me" (p. 320f.).

All that Nanda has to convey to her mother can be put in two or three sentences. Yet James insists on the allusive and the misunderstood to draw out the conversation. An occasional exchange of this kind is quite palatable when the situation requires it, but a diet of page upon page is cloying.[8]

It would be most unfair, however, with these remarks to write off *The Awkward Age* as a simple failure. There was more to James's attempt than the novel's special techniques. The *Age* is, as Percy Lubbock has explained, a novel about an inevitable contingency that befalls some fashionable London families:

> . . . Periodically it must happen that their young grow up; the daughter of the house reaches the "awkward age," becomes suddenly too old for the schoolroom and joins her elders below. Then comes the difficulty; there is an interval in which she is still too young for the freedom of her elders's style, and it looks as though she might disconcert them not a little, sitting there with wide eyes. Do they simply disregard her and continue their game as before? Do they try to adapt their style to her inexperience? Apparently they have no theory of their proper course; the difficulty seems to strike them afresh, every time that it recurs. In other such worlds, not of modern London, it is foreseen and provided for; the young woman is married and launched at once, there is no awkward age. But here and now—or rather here and *then*, in the nineteenth century—it makes a real little situation, and this is the subject of Henry James's book.[9]

This problem is the center of a world which in its principles and values is so kaleidoscopically ironic that the work could almost be—as its principal events testify—a *fin de siècle Beggar's Opera*.[10]

The Awkward Age is a novel which thrives on the unusual. An adulterous guardian (the Duchess) rears in innocence a niece (Aggie), who later contends with her for her lover (Petherton). A sophisticated mother (Mrs. Brook) rears a daughter (Nanda), who later threatens her intimacy with a handsome bachelor (Vanderbank). The same delicately urbane lady, who desires her daughter's marriage to a man of means, prevents the realization of it in the most vulgar way open to her. The same girl, morally irreproachable—in spite of being raised in an atmosphere where the risqué is the rule rather than the exception—frightens off possible suitors because of what she knows. A wealthy gentleman (Mitchy), who wants to marry this knowledgeable girl, marries, on her advice, the innocent girl who subsequently becomes promiscuous. His troubles then unite him with the girl he loves in a way that was formerly impossible. A poor young man (Vanderbank) refuses to marry the attractive and knowledgeable young girl who loves him and marriage to whom will bring him a fortune. A disgruntled husband (Mr. Cashmore) is weaned from a love affair (with Carrie Donner) by the counsels of a young girl (Nanda) whose brother (Harold) becomes a social success by having an affair with the man's wife (Fanny Cashmore). An older man (Longdon), who paternally loves the knowledge-able young girl and is willing to give her up and handsomely endow her, is the one who finally wins the young girl—and he retains his fortune. Thus the society which forms the young girl implicitly rejects her because of her knowledge and accepts the formerly innocent girl because her new "freedom" provides it material for conversation. And, finally, the old and traditional world, represented by the older man, alone accepts for her own value the knowledgeable girl who is the peculiar product of that radically modern society in which neither he nor she can have a meaningful life.

To realize this world of paradoxical events and compounded frustrations, James chose a method in which he sought to test his reader's perceptiveness. By presenting the ironic incidents which clarify his central subject without recourse to anything more than a reporter as centre of vision, he forced the reader into the position of a judge of moral, social, and, consequently, literary values. As has been noted, James at times failed to make those scenes which develop and reflect the central prob-lem relate precisely to it. But at times he succeeded. And per-haps no other scene testifies so well to James's ability to realize his world of complex confusion as does Chapter XXX in the "Tishy Grendon" section of the novel—one requiring quotation at some length here prior to analysis.

"Is his wife in the other room?" Mrs. Brook now put to Tishy.

Tishy, after a stare about, recovered the acuter consciousness to account for this guest. "Oh yes—she's playing with him."

"But with whom, dear?"

"Why, with Petherton. I thought you knew."

"Knew they're playing—?" Mrs. Brook was almost Socratic.

"The Missus is regularly wound up," her husband meanwhile, without resonance, observed to Vanderbank.

"Brilliant indeed!" Vanderbank replied.

"But she's rather naughty, you know," Edward after a pause continued.

"Oh fiendish!" his interlocutor said with a short smothered laugh that might have represented for a spectator a sudden start at such a flash of analysis from such a quarter.

When Vanderbank's attention at any rate was free again their hostess, assisted to the transition, was describing the play, as she called it, of the absentees. "She has hidden a book and he's trying to find it."

"Hide and seek? Why, isn't it innocent, Mitch!" Mrs. Brook exclaimed.

Mitchy, speaking for the first time, faced her with extravagant gloom. "Do you really think so?"

"That's *her* innocence!" the Duchess laughed to him.

"And don't you suppose he has found it *yet*?"

. . . .

"He can't," Tishy said with simplicity.

"But why in the world—?"

"You see she's sitting on it"—Tishy felt, it was plain, the responsibility of explanation. "So unless he pulls her off—"

. . . .

Lord Petherton, arriving with animation and followed so swiftly by his young companion that she presented herself as pursuing him, shook triumphantly over his head a small volume in blue paper. There was a general movement at the sight of them, and by the time they had rejoined their friends the company, pushing back seats and causing a variety of mute expression smoothly to circulate, was pretty well on its feet. "See—he *has* pulled her off!" said Mrs. Brook.

Little Aggie, to whom plenty of pearls were singularly becoming, met it as pleasant sympathy. "Yes, and it was a *real* pull. . . ."

Mrs. Brook's sympathy passed, however, with no great ease from Aggie's pearls to her other charms; fixing the former indeed so markedly that Harold had a quick word about it for Lady Fanny. "When poor mummy thinks, you know, that Nanda might have had them—!

Lady Fanny's attention, for that matter, had resisted them as little. "Well, I dare say that if I had wanted *I* might!"

"Lord—*could* you have stood him?" the young man returned. "But I believe women can stand anything!" he profoundly concluded. His mother meanwhile, recovering herself, had begun to ejaculate on the prints in Aggie's arms, and he was then diverted from the sense of what he "personally," as he would have said, couldn't have stood, by a glance at Lord Petherton's trophy, for which he made a prompt grab. "The bone of contention?" Lord

Petherton had let it go and Harold remained arrested by the cover. "Why blest if it hasn't Van's name!"

"Van's?"—his mother was near enough to effect her own snatch, after which she swiftly faced the proprietor of the volume. "Dear man, it's the last thing you lent me! But I don't think," she added, turning to Tishy, "that I ever passed such a production on to *you*."

"It was just seeing Mr. Van's hand," Aggie conscientiously explained, "that made me think one was free—!"

"But it isn't Mr. Van's hand!"—Mrs. Brook quite smiled at the error. She thrust the book straight at Mr. Longdon. "*Is* that Mr. Van's hand?"

Holding the disputed object, which he had put on his nippers to glance at, he presently, without speaking, looked over these aids straight at Nanda, who looked as straight back at him. "It was I who wrote Mr. Van's name." The girl's eyes were on Mr. Longdon, but her words as for the company. "I brought the book here from Buckingham Crescent and left it by accident in the other room."

"By accident, my dear," her mother replied, "I do quite hope. But what on earth did you bring it for? It's too hideous."

Nanda seemed to wonder. "Is it?" she murmured.

"Then you haven't read it?"

She just hesitated. "One hardly knows now, I think, what is and what isn't."

"She brought it only for *me* to read," Tishy gravely interposed.

Mrs. Brook looked strange. "Nanda recommended it?"

"Oh no—the contrary." Tishy, as if scared by so much publicity, floundered a little. "She only told me—"

"The awful subject?" Mrs. Brook wailed.

There was no deepening an echo of the drollery of this last passage that it was a minute before Vanderbank could be heard saying: "The responsibility's wholly mine for setting the beastly thing in motion. Still," he added good-humouredly and as to minimise if not the cause at least the consequence, "I think I agree with Nanda that it's no worse than anything else."

Mrs. Brook had recovered the volume from Mr. Longdon's relaxed hand and now, without another glance at it, held it behind her with an unusual air of firmness. "Oh how can you say that, my dear man, of anything so revolting?"

The discussion kept them for the instant well face to face. "Then did *you* read it?"

She debated, jerking the book into the nearest empty chair, where Mr. Cashmore quickly pounced on it. "Wasn't it for that you brought it me?" she demanded. Yet before he could answer she again challenged her child. "Have you read this work, Nanda?"

"Yes mamma."

"Oh I say!" cried Mr. Cashmore, hilarious and turning the leaves.

Mr. Longdon had by this time ceremoniously approached Tishy. "Good-night" (pp. 424-433).

In its own way this scene epitomizes what James wanted *The Awkward Age* to be. Note here that there is no flaccidly irrelevant conversation about the past or the future. This scene is irrevocably involved with the present. Speech flashes from event and event from speech. The romp of Aggie and Petherton perdures through the conversation and produces it so that the physical movement and the conversation capture the essence of the novel's complex situation. Here Nanda and Aggie are set in a society of which they are part. The society itself is degenerate. It is composed of unscrupulous parents and guardians, unhappily married couples, sexually promiscuous individuals, social parasites, the victimized, and the simply stupid. All these show themselves in the conversation and events of the scene. The romp of Aggie and Petherton is a key to a far from innocent relationship, one that Mitchy as the unhappy husband must stand by and witness. The central social symbol of moral decay here, Van's novel, reflects the decay of manners and the social hypocrisy of a predaceous amoral society. Thus Mrs. Brook's feigned excitement is merely a social camouflage for her predatory way of alienating Van from Nanda and securing Mr. Longdon's future support of her daughter. She no more cares that Nanda has read Van's novel than she does that the girl has read "Goldilocks." The point is that she here creates a scene which will so disgust Longdon that in his affection for Nanda—seeing her abandoned by Van —he will eventually ask her to come to him and take her out of a society where such vulgarity is possible. And if this characterizes Mrs. Brook's unscrupulous use of people, Mr. Cashmore's pouncing on the novel signals his turn of mind, Harold's remark to Fanny points to the intimacy of their relation and to his eye for money and her attitude toward opportunity, Edward's quip reflects his general inanity, Van's remarks his vacuousness, and Mitchy's his plight. Aside from Nanda, the only one in the room who shows a grain of sense is Longdon, and he does it with a traditional and polite "Goodnight."

This scene is everything that James could have hoped for. There is a central symbol, the French novel, tying together two strands of value evident in an hypocrisy which allows Aggie to be a social success and Nanda to be a social failure.[11] It provides a chance for comment or action or both by each member of Tishy's party. And as these comments and actions

92

contribute to the scene they simultaneously characterize the speakers and doers. James produces in small a central situation surrounded by reflectors; he produces, in other words, a capsule form of what he wanted his whole novel to be.

The scene, while being as objective as any in the novel, is so without sacrificing intensity and economy. Like the Kensington Gardens scene in *Maisie,* this episode has action in the foreground and in the background; while one thing happens before the reader's eyes, the amount of his wonderment increases as reports of what is happening out of earshot are given. When foreground and background actions merge, they center on the French novel which focuses the comments and movements of the characters. Finally, this scene, plumbing the depths of the present, reaches to the past and future as well. Not only has Mrs. Brook discussed this novel with Van earlier, but she has also been trying to get Nanda a place far from her own fiscally impoverished side. Now with the novel as her tool she resolutely sets about her task. The success of her venture is witnessed in the last chapter of the novel, where that society which is incapable of placing its natural offspring is measured with the fullness of irony by an old man who alone is human enough to understand what its illustrious representative, Vanderbank, cannot:

"Come!" he then very firmly said—quite indeed as if it were a question of their moving on the spot.

It literally made her smile, which, with a certain compunction, she immediately corrected by doing for him in the pressure of her lips to his cheek what he had just done for herself. "To-day?" she more seriously asked.

He looked at his watch. "To-morrow."

She paused, but clearly for assent. "That's what I mean by your taking me as I am. It *is,* you know, for a girl—extraordinary."

"Oh I know what it is!" he exclaimed with an odd fatigue in his tenderness.

But she continued, with the shadow of her scruple, to explain. "We're many of us, we're most of us—as you long ago saw and showed you felt—extraordinary now. We can't help it. It isn't really our fault. There's so much else that's extraordinary that if we're in it all so much *we* must naturally be." It was all obviously clearer to her than ever yet, and her sense of it found renewed expression; so that she might have been, as she wound up, a very much older person than her friend. "Everything's different from what it used to be."

"Yes, everything," he returned with an air of final indoctrination. "That's what he ought to have recognised."

"As *you* have?" Nanda was once more—and completely now—enthroned in high justice. "Oh he's more old-fashioned than you."

"Much more," said Mr. Longdon with a queer face (pp. 543f.)

Anticipated by so much that precedes it and finding the fulfillment of final irony in the conversation between Nanda and Longdon, the "Tishy Grendon" scene is obviously one that reverberates in many directions, setting up with the greatest economy possible a psychological and structural intensity in an episode rigorous in its objectivity.

What this scene mirrors is the complex meaning of *The Awkward Age* itself; for the novel, like this one episode, is concerned with a group of people who have created a society in which it is impossible to live a meaningful life. It projects modern frustration in scenes where the young and the old, the traditional and the contemporary, the intelligent and the ignorant rigorously contend with each other in seeking the satisfactory. The world of the *Age* is one in which social convention has become so complex that the truly human, lost in vacuous details, can no longer be found in married love but only in the paternal affection of an old man for a crying girl. If, as must be admitted, James was not completely successful in shaping a form totally adequate to this meaning, it is well to remember that the breadth of meaning itself, and those occasional scenes in which it is carefully structured, witness and in a way justify the limited achievement of *The Awkward Age* as an experiment in objectivity.

5

The Sacred Fount
and the Perspective of Achievement

James's *The Sacred Fount* has been for many years a continual source of suggestive critical befuddlement. It has found its way into different genres: parody, autobiography, parable, primer, psychological detective story, and even Greek tragedy. Its subject has been variously taken to be vampirism, art and life, human relationships, James's disillusionment, the artist *manqué,* and the Archimago image. *The Sacred Fount* has been placed in the tradition of novels of ambiguity, the theory of art, autobiography, ghostly tales, and short stories.[1] To some it is a novel with a perfect form; to others it is a literary monstrosity.[2] However, in the process of *The Sacred Fount's* becoming this much-judged and much-interpreted work, many facts relevant to both its meaning and its dramatic effect seem to have been overlooked.

Most readers have approached the novel by attempting to find out the truth about the Brissendens, Lady John, Gilbert Long, and May Server. Nothing could be more precisely wrong than this tack, which is inevitably taken in vain. It is impossible to determine the truth about these relationships; moreover, if the reader were able to determine it, the novel would be a failure. What makes the *Fount* so different from the novels which just preceded it and from earlier ones like *Roderick Hudson, The American, The Portrait,* and so forth, is that they depend on one's eventually knowing what really happened, while the *Fount* does not. The difference for some has become an insurmountable difficulty, and the *Fount* either has been praised for what it is not or has been written off as a failure. This is unfortunate because the novel in its own small way is really quite perfect.

In reading *The Sacred Fount,* one should center his interest on what the narrator and Grace Brissenden present as happening. It does not really matter whether their theories of events correspond with the events. The novel is not a problem in metaphysics; it is, rather, a study in logic and semiosis. The *Fount* is not concerned with truth, but with the correct reasoning about signs. That the meaning ascribed to the signs conforms with the objective reality is impossible to determine because of the deliberate ambiguity of the novel. The focus of the novel is not the true relation persisting among the Brissendens, Long, May Server, and Lady John. The centre of composition in the novel is formed by the logical constructions which the narrator and Grace Brissenden fit together from signs that are identical but that mean something different to each of them. The *Fount* presents a limited number of these signs: Grace Brissenden's youthful appearance, Gilbert Long's social ease, Guy Brissenden's aged appearance, May Server's association with different men, Lady John's strained wit, and some few others. Mrs. Brissenden and the narrator interpret the meanings of these signs in distinctly different ways, and they incorporate the different meanings they arrive at into divergent logical constructions. When all the signs are fitted into these two separate and symmetrical constructs, the novel ends. The narrator has used up all the signs available to him and incorporated them into his system. Grace Brissenden has used up the same signs and incorporated them into her system. There are no more signs to use and there are no more characters with systems. With everything used and nothing left over the ultimate relativity of "objective reality" stands in evidence, and the novel has come to its logically ambiguous conclusion.

If *The Sacred Fount* is to be read well, then, it is necessary to rest easy with ambiguity, because if there were no ambiguity, there would be no novel. James indeed signals this to his reader in the opening sentences of the *Fount*:

> It was an occasion, I felt—the prospect of a large party— to look out at the station for others, possible friends and even possible enemies, who might be going. Such premonitions, it was true, bred fears when they failed to breed hopes, though it was to be added that there were sometimes, in the case, rather happy ambiguities. One was glowered at, in the compartment, by people who on the morrow, after breakfast, were to prove charming; one was spoken to first by people whose sociability was subsequently to show as bleak; and one built with confidence on others who were never to reappear at all—who were only going to Birmingham.[3]

Gilbert Long, the first of the signs to appear in the novel, is introduced immediately after the passage quoted above. A few sentences later, he is followed by the appearance of a second sign in the person of Grace Brissenden. Long, whom the narrator had always taken as stupid, now appears to him to be intelligent; and Grace, who formerly had a rather middle-aged appearance, now seems to the narrator so youthful that he, in fact, does not at first recognize her. What, indeed, the narrator asks, do these signs—the intelligent Long and the young Grace —mean? He enters into conversation with each to find out something about the other. He speaks with Long about Grace. The narrator professes that she has grown younger since her marriage to Guy Brissenden. Long maintains that Grace has just not grown any older since her marriage; that, indeed, she has remained the same. With this brief discussion finished, the reader now has a sign and two meanings for it: Grace Brissenden looks quite young either because she has grown younger or because she has not aged since her marriage. It is impossible to determine which reason is the true one.

While Long is occupied with a newsboy, the narrator discusses him with Mrs. Brissenden. "She put it to me frankly," he says, "that she had never seen a man so improved: a confidence that I met with alacrity, as it showed me that, under the same impression, I had not been astray" (p. 8). She professes to know why Long has changed:

"Well, a very clever woman has for some time past——"

"Taken"—this beginning was of course enough—"a particular interest in him? Do you mean Lady John?" I inquired; and, as she evidently did, I rather demurred. "Do you call Lady John a very clever woman?"

"Surely. That's why I kindly arranged that, as she was to take, I happened to learn, the next train, Guy should come with her" (p. 9).

The narrator, however, rejects Lady John's candidacy after he meets her; she is not intelligent enough, in his opinion, to supply Long with a quantity of wit. He also meets Guy Brissenden, who appears to him to have aged considerably. Ford Obert, an artist friend, corroborates his observation: "Why had so fine a young creature married a man three times her age? He was of course astounded when I told him the young creature was much nearer three times Brissenden's . . ." (p. 28). The ensuing conversation gives the narrator a chance to present his view of the relation:

Mrs. Briss had to get her new blood, her extra allowance of time and bloom, somewhere; and from whom could she so conveniently extract them as from Guy himself?

She *has*, by an extraordinary feat of legerdemain, extracted them; and he, on his side, to supply her, has had to tap the sacred fount. But the sacred fount is like the greedy man's description of the turkey as an "awkward" dinner dish. It may be sometimes too much for a single share, but it's not enough to go round" (p. 29).

The reader has now another sign: Guy looks as old as Grace looks young. (And like Grace's youth, Guy's aged appearance has the corroboration of someone other than the narrator.[4]) The reader is also put in possession of the narrator's theory of relationship between the husband and wife—a theory which has a certain logic to it in that it fits the signs. But it is impossible to determine whether the theory represents the true meanings of the signs.

Chapter III of the novel finds the narrator together again with Mrs. Brissenden, with whom he discusses the improbability of Lady John's supplying Long with any amount of intelligence. Grace then suggests May Server as a substitute, but the narrator is dissatisfied with her as well. Grace presses for the candidacy of Mrs. Server while the narrator insists that they look for someone else. The remainder of the novel largely consists in Mrs. Brissenden's and the narrator's attempts to find some woman who has the prerequisites to serve as Gilbert Long's source of intelligence. When the narrator comes finally to recognize the suitability of May Server, he refuses to allow Mrs. Brissenden knowledge of this. He, in fact, takes to protecting May—to "seeing her through."

As events continue to develop, familiarities are noted between May Server and Guy Brissenden, Gilbert Long and Grace Brissenden. In his passion for system and symmetry, the narrator theorizes that May Server : Gilbert Long :: Guy Brissenden : Grace Brissenden, and that May : Guy :: Long : Grace. He sees May and Guy as seeking mutual comfort in each other's company while Long and Grace ally to protect their gains.

With his system developed, the narrator spends his time trying to help May. He does not want to see her compromised by Grace Brissenden. It happens, however, that Grace makes an about-face and presents the narrator with a new arrangement of alliances. She now holds that Gilbert Long is as dull as he ever was and that consequently Lady John is really to be seen as his consort. Lady John, in her theory, will not have had to sacrifice an iota of intelligence because Gilbert Long will not have gained even that much. Grace also holds that May Server is making love to Guy while trying to cover her tracks by associating with other men.

The novel draws to an end, then, with both the narrator and Grace Brissenden using all the available signs but with each of them formulating a different logical system of meanings from them. With neither the narrator nor Mrs. Brissenden apparently able to convince the other of the truth of his view, the novel ends. The situation that confronts them proves itself truly analogous to the sacred fount of the narrator's definition and the novel's title: it provides too much for each to handle separately and too little for both to handle collectively.

Some critics, however, have been quick to say that Grace Brissenden's presentation of the situation represents the reality which destroys the narrator's theory.[5] It represents that overdose of reality which James found harmful to art. Thus art is destroyed by too much reality.[6] Interpreters, consequently, have misconstrued what is actually criticism of Grace Brissenden and her system as condescension to that system on the part of the narrator. What is forgotten is that the narrator, who is shielding May Server, cannot tell Mrs. Brissenden what he actually suspects May's relation to Long to be. And since Grace depends so much as fitting an "awfully sharp" May

Server into her system, that system is really ridiculous to the narrator, who realizes, but does not admit, that May is *not* so "awfully sharp." Also, careful reading shows that Mrs. Brissenden has supposedly learned about Guy and May only after making her midnight appointment with the narrator, and thus that she could not have intended to meet him to combat his theory in the manner that she does.[7] And, finally, before Grace has ever fitted her final piece into place, the narrator has decided that she has come to him in order to lie.[8] As long as he maintains such a position, his statements must be interpreted in the light of it. The reason that he is disconcerted at the end of the *Fount* is quite clear: "What I too fatally lacked was her tone" (p. 319). And her "tone," as the reader has just learned, was one of "insolence" (p. 318).[9]

Any consistent reading of the novel, then, must accept the ultimate ambiguity of the *Fount,* the ultimate impossibility of determining the truth of the matter, and the ultimate importance of the equiprobable schemes of relations drawn up by Grace Brissenden and the narrator. Whatever superstructure of interpretation is to be finally raised must stand firm on a fundamental recognition that the *Fount* is, basically, a novel which represents the process of imaginative fabrication of a "structure" from a "germ" that has been conceived as a "subject." The fascination of *The Sacred Fount* lies in the building of the structure; the climax of the novel comes when Grace Brissenden faces the narrator with another structure which opposes his. And the book ends with the reader's looking at two structures, neither of which he can choose with certainty, but both of which he has reason to regard as probable.

In the process of giving *The Sacred Fount* its characterizing ambiguity, James did not forfeit his interest in the novel's dramatic dimension. In the *Fount,* in fact, he strained to the utmost his ability to realize dramatic qualities through the symmetrical structure of an action represented in scenes and pictures, composed around a centre, and focused through the vision of the narrator.

As was noted, the novel is concerned primarily with the interpretation of a certain few events. This naturally tends to focus interest on the interpreting consciousness of the narrator.[10] The narrator begins his fictional existence with that bent for observation, interpretation and system that obsesses him throughout the novel.[11] This combines, in the course of events, with his regard for May Server and the attitude of defense he adopts toward her. Laboring under these dual pressures, the narrator stands as the prime source of psychological intensity. This intensity, resulting from his dual obsession for system and defense, is intimately dependent on the novel's structure. *The Fount* depends upon the narrator's building up his symmetrical picture of the situation at Newmarch, as the novel's vocabulary clearly shows.[12] The picture must compose; no fact can exist in the novel that cannot be assimilated into his design. When everything fits, the picture is perfect and the narrator's job of work is finished. The fact that each of the narrator's pieces also fills out Grace Brissenden's picture is not inimical to the novel as a symmetrically realized work, but rather demonstrates the flexibility of a novel, governed by a principle of ambiguity, that allows in its over-all construction for two smaller symmetries either of which in its own way is satisfactory and both of which combine to give the *Fount* its pictorial balance.[13]

Of course, the fact that both the narrator and Mrs. Brissenden can arrive simultaneously at two systems of equally probable meanings from a single set of signs shows the extent to which economy is operative in this novel. The number of signs available to the narrator, Mrs. Brissenden, and their artist

friend Ford Obert is minimal. For this reason the economy of
The Sacred Fount develops in a structure that is, in a way,
music-like. In fact, it seems to find a most satisfactory analogy
in the structure of the fugue, a musical form in which a *subject* ("a scrap of melody") undergoes continuous expansion
through the *counterpoint* ("interweaving of melodies") of different *voices*. If there are two subjects, the form is called a
double fugue. Very generally, the fugue usually comprises
exposition(s), voices treating the subject; *episode(s)*, voices
treating some motif or motifs from the subject; and a *coda*,
which returns to the subject. The coda may end with a *stretto*,
a combination of the appearances of the subject, for added effect.[14]

The structure of *The Sacred Fount* becomes quite intelligible in a comparison with that of a double fugue. The two
subjects are the youth of Grace Brissenden with its possible
source and the intelligence of Gilbert Long with its possible
source. The two subjects are developed in a series of *exposi-
tions* which lead the narrator, with the help of Grace Brissenden and Ford Obert (as second and third *voices*), to decide
that Grace : Guy :: Long : "X."[15] "X" becomes variously Lady
John and May Server. The *episodes* in the fugue-like structure
are found in the novel's various motifs: Guy's and May's association with each other, the connection between Grace and
Long, the role of the narrator as counselor and silent confidant.
The *coda* begins in Chapter XII and ends with Chapter XIV
in a *stretto* in which the narrator persists in his view of the
subject while Grace Brissenden simultaneously, so to speak,
plays a different melody with notes from the same subject.
Thus very much is made from very little as economy flows
from the structure of the subjects.

It is a paradox in a way that the *Fount* should also revel in
objectivity. James, who was seldom satisfied with a first-person

narrator in a novel, overcame the dangers of subjectivity with his system of signs. The reader who sees the novel only as a series of interpretations misses a salient point. The narrator's theory is challanged by Grace Brissenden's and both depend on a series of signs: Long as intelligent, Grace as young, Guy as old, and so forth. Whether one wants to accept either theory of meanings is entirely up to him; but the fact is that neither seems to have more validity than the other. James appeals in the *Fount*—as he did in so strikingly different a manner in *The Awkward Age*—to the intelligence of the reader. The final tribunal of judgment is neither the narrator's intelligence nor Grace Brissenden's, but rather the reader's own. And for him the "objective situation" seems to remain one of complete relativity.

In conclusion, one can say that minimally *The Sacred Fount* is a catch-all of what James had tried to make the dramatic novel before the "major phase." In it the gradual shift of focus from event to consciousness of event finds an apogee. The imaginative art of building rather than the actuality built on assumes central significance. Also, in the *Fount* the inhuman use of one's fellow creatures, a theme dramatized in *The Spoils of Poynton, What Maisie Knew,* and *The Awkward Age,* finds symbolic realization in the narrator's theory of the sacred fount and the complex relations persisting between human beings who seem to him to draw physical and mental energy from their fellows. Finally, the *Fount* shows a fitting culmination of the constructional passion for symmetrical effect that has been traced in *Maisie, Poynton,* and the *Age.* Here, in fact, the novel finds its resolution in the unresolved conflict of those schemes which perfect its ambiguity. Whether the *Fount* is more than what is sketched here and than what has been detailed above is a moot point. Though critics have seen it in various ways, under different lights, and have tailored many interpretations of cuts different from the one presented here, it would seem that the *Fount*'s dramatic dimensions, its structural complexity and, above all, its skeletal ambiguity must be recognized and measured before it can be comfortably and profitably fitted out in any of the many-colored coats of interpretation.

The Sacred Fount, like the other major novels of the middle period, has not infrequently been objected to because of some strangeness in its structure or its meaning or both. James's contemporary readers considered it a "making of nothing out of nothing," and, consequently, "as brilliant a stupid piece of work as Mr. James has ever done. . . ." Richard Foley notes that in the judgments of James's reviewers "more disappointment than usual and some disgust were evident."[16] F. W. Dupee, surveying present trends, reports that the *Fount* is still seen as one of those novels that have been "widely regarded" as products "of a misguided virtuosity."[17] It seems quite obvious from these remarks that the serious failure to see this novel and those preceding it as entities and in a perspective has yielded the singularly unfortunate concentration of attention on what seems to be aberrant in their structure and meaning. Few suppositions, indeed, seem quite so divisive and invidious as that which more or less tacitly attributes a reader's misunderstanding to the author's failure to achieve a satisfactory literary structure. As a counter to such an assumption, it has been suggested that as experiments in the "dramatic novel" *The Spoils of Poynton, What Maisie Knew,* and *The Sacred Fount* are successful novels. They realize through a careful application of developed narrative techniques those qualities of intensity, economy, and objectivity which James considered dramatic. Each has an esthetic integrity deriving from a structure that dramatizes its action. It is for this reason that *The Awkward Age*—so daring in conception and so brilliant in parts—is satisfying only to the degree that it realizes its dramatic potential. These novels are, then, esthetically fine to the degree that they are dramatically rendered; their dramatic technique is a recognized part of their excellence. With an understanding, then, of James's theory of the dramatic novel and with some appreciation of the literary value of *Poynton, Maisie,* the *Age,* and the *Fount,* it would seem well to conclude by touching, though briefly, on another dimension of their importance—their relation to James's late novels.

Unlike the early and late novels, the middle novels are by and large devoted to the London scene. Such recognized early works as *Roderick Hudson, The American,* and *Portrait of a Lady,* to say nothing of *The Wings of the Dove, The Ambassadors* and *The Golden Bowl* in the late period, treat the international theme—the effect of Europe on the American abroad. It would be naïve to suppose that the late novels are simply a sum of the early themes and the middle methods. One cannot quite add *Roderick* to *Maisie* and get *The Ambassadors.* Nevertheless, the middle novels as dramatic novels have contributed much to the recognized achievement of the "major phase."

The character of the intensity in *The Golden Bowl,* for instance, is already visible in *The Spoils of Poynton.* Whereas the former novel has five different centres of vision, its second book is largely devoted to Maggie Verver's vision of events. Abstracting from details, it is quite evident that Maggie's problems are much like Fleda's before her. Once Maggie learns about the relation between Charlotte and the Prince, she sets out to separate them. She must do this, however, by regaining the love of Amerigo and without allowing her father and Charlotte to know precisely what she knows and what she is doing. Like Fleda Vetch, then, she is centrally placed in order to save a situation. Both heroines accomplish their tasks through the application of a system of ethics in which the end justifies the means and in which lying and the pawn-like manipulation of others are acceptable parts of the game. Each young woman has an enormous amount of responsibility and each has more information than any other character in her respective novel. Their business becomes one of masking the truth and displaying only select information. The hero-ines, in short, must play the game of appearance and reality with all subtlety. Each is ultimately successful in her task: Fleda sees Owen's "honor" preserved and Maggie regains the love of her husband. In the use of centres of vision and the manipulation of appearance and reality for the sake of maxi-mum intensity, and in the tasks they exact from and the pres-sures they place upon their heroines, few novels seem closer to each other than *The Spoils of Poynton* and *The Golden Bowl.*

What Maisie Knew and *The Ambassadors* complement each other in the same areas as *Poynton* and the *Bowl,* for in them the use of centres of vision and appearance and reality is quite similar. In *Maisie,* the precocious little girl sees all that hap-pens but does not understand it. The narrator is there—"go-ing behind," as James puts it—to make sure that the reader does understand, but as the novel draws to its close and Maisie both sees and understands, the task of the narrator is mini-mized. Maisie assumes a role akin to Strether's. Strether needs no one to interpret for him. His experience of Paris becomes the reader's. But in another sense he is like Maisie; he too has something to learn; and for him, as for her, the convergence of appearance and reality is the crux of experience. That Madame de Vionnet is Chad Newsome's mistress is as impor-tant a fact to Strether as Sir Claude's fear of Mrs. Beale is to Maisie. Whereas Maisie's adventure ends with her knowledge,

Strether's in a sense begins again; but for both Maisie and Strether there have been, through a gradual understanding of the meaning of appearances, pragmatic adventures in the acquisition of experience.

The continuous changing and squaring off of relationships that constitute the symmetry of *The Golden Bowl* are later reflections of James's idea of the novel's being as carefully composed and balanced as a painting. The *Bowl,* certainly, in this respect is closer to *The Sacred Fount* than to any other earlier novel. But the *Fount,* too, resembles *The Wings of the Dove* in the sense that in both novels one scheme of relations is finally challenged by another. Just as in the *Fount* Grace Brissenden can build up a new system of meanings from the same signs that the narrator uses for his system, so too in the *Wings* the very elements calculated to foster the love of Kate and Merton finally bring it to smash. The novel ends with Milly's letter burning in the fireplace—a letter which was to anticipate the happiness of Merton and Kate but whose charred remains clearly symbolize its impossibility. If the structure of *The Wings of the Dove* finds some anticipation in *The Sacred Fount,* its motifs seem clearly related to *The Awkward Age.* In both novels a girl (Nanda, Kate) is victimized by a dominating woman (Mrs. Brook, Maud Lowder) and a feckless father (Mr. Brook, Mr. Croy). Each girl fails to succeed at a crucial moment: Nanda is unable to win the love of Van; Kate is unable to marry Merton. Each consequently is faced with an unsatisfactory compromise: Nanda is forced to live in a "free circle" of society where the knowledge she gains will make her unacceptable to any suitor; Kate must use Merton to get Milly's money, and to do so she must sacrifice her honor by visiting his rooms. The final effect for both is the same: they lose the man they love because of the compromises they were led to make at a moment of expediency.

The three novels of the "major phase" are constructed in a series of scenes and pictures. Both *Poynton* and *Maisie* anticipate this structure, but the *Age* and the *Fount,* respectively, show the lengths to which scene and picture can be developed. The *Age* is especially important in demonstrating the systematic use of different points of view that conversation provides. Though James never again pressed the value of this technique as he did in the *Age,* he did make use of Susan Stringham, Maria Gostrey and Fanny Assingham in ways which suggest, in their conversations in the respective novels, lamps being trained on a central object. The extraordinary introspection of the narrator of *The Sacred Fount* also served to show James the possibilities inherent in the structural use of picture. There was only one step from the *Fount'*s first-person narrator to the complex third-person point of view of Strether, whose existence, like the Narrator's in the *Fount,* was so much occupied with seeking the meanings for signs.

It is true, of course, that James's late novels connect with his early as well as with his middle ones. Part of the situation of *The Portrait of a Lady* is duplicated in *The Golden Bowl.* There is in evidence in both novels the resumption of an affair between a married man and a former lover when he finds his wife's affections insufficient to satisfy his own. Again, in *Portrait,* certainly, there is found something of the theme of *The Wings.* Both novels concern a rich girl whose love is sought for the sake of her money. In each case the supposed lover is acting in the interest of another woman. Further, few novels could be compared so easily as *Roderick* and *The Ambassadors.* In the former there is the story of Hudson's romance with Christina Light, his eventual failure in love, and his death. Also, there is the story of Rowland Mallet's moral development when he is beset by the problems of Roderick's conduct. And Mallet's love for Mary Garland is not to be forgotten.

The Ambassadors shows the same general structure in the story of Newsome's affair with Madame de Vionnet, and in Strether's reaction as his relation to the guilty parties becomes clear to himself. There is in addition Strether's relation to Maria Gostrey, ultimately as hopeless as the Mallet-Garland one in *Roderick*. In these later novels, then, there is some reflection of James's early period.

It would be impossible, however, even to think of the *Wings, Ambassadors,* and the *Bowl,* no matter how close their relation to the early novels could be shown to be, without James's middle period. It was in this period that the use of centre of vision was subtlized, that the stage of action shifted more and more to the consciousness of characters, that symmetrical patterning developed to the point of structuring ironic reversals, that the conception of action was simplified while its development was made more complex, that the centres of vision at times came near to being centres of composition, that the use of scenes and pictures was perfected, and that the style of the late novels was anticipated in the introspective narrator of *The Sacred Fount*. Since it is impossible to imagine *The Wings of the Dove, The Ambassadors* and *The Golden Bowl* without their characters of exquisite sensibilities, without their complex development, without their symmetry and their irony, without their alternation of scenes and pictures, without, in short, all that is anticipated by *The Spoils of Poynton, What Maisie Knew, The Awkward Age* and *The Sacred Fount,* it is impossible readily to imagine James's "major phase" without these dramatic novels of the middle period, which, by their independent esthetic value as well as their influence on the late novels, constitute something of a "minor phase."

111

Notes

CHAPTER 1

[1] Book III, 349C in Alan H. Gilbert's translation in his edition *Literary Criticism: Plato to Dryden* (New York, 1940), p. 38.

[2] 1448a20-23 in Bywater's translation.

[3] Among the more famous conversions of forms are *Daisy Miller, The American,* and *The Other House,* but the *nouvelle* known today as "The Covering End" had the most complex history. It was first a play (*Summersoft*), then a *nouvelle* ("The Covering End"), and finally a play again (*The High Bid*). For details see *The Complete Plays of Henry James,* ed. Leon Edel (London, 1949); hereafter referred to as *Plays.*

[4] *The Method of Henry James* (Philadelphia, 1954), pp. lxxixf.; hereafter referred to as *Method.*

[5] *The Modern Fables of Henry James* (Cambridge, Mass., 1935), p. 37.

[6] Christy Morgan Taylor disagrees with this opinion. "For James," he writes, "the dramatic form depended wholly on the spoken word and therefore was inimical to the novel as picture." "The Pictorial Element in the Theory and Practice of Henry James" (diss. Stanford, 1955), p. 158. This, however, seems false. Thus James: " 'Dialogue,' as it is commonly called, is singularly suicidal from the moment it is not directly illustrative of something given us by another method, something constituted and presented." *Notes on Novelists* (London, 1914), p. 350; hereafter referred to as *Notes.* See also the more considered remark of Rene Wellek: "Dialogue is only a means toward a general effect which James often calls the 'picture'. . . ." "Henry James's Literary Theory and Criticism," *American Literature,* XXX (1958), 311. Leo T. Hendrick, "Henry James: The Late and Early Styles: A Stylistics Study" (diss. Michigan, 1953), p. 48 *et passim* in Chapter II. Hendrick shows conclusively that any remark like Taylor's is ill-advised, and that both dialogue and non-dialogue form the whole of the dramatized novel.

[7] *The Art of the Novel: Critical Prefaces,* ed. R. P. Blackmur (New York, 1957), p. 15; hereafter referred to as *Prefaces.*

[8] *The Scenic Art, Notes on Acting and Drama: 1872-1901,* ed. Allan Wade (New York, 1957), p. 7; hereafter referred to as *Scenic Art.*

[9] *Prefaces,* p. 276.

[10] *Scenic Art,* p. 276.

[11] *Ibid.,* p. 252.

[12] *Ibid.,* p. 254.

[13] *Ibid.,* p. 255. For the general relation of James to Ibsen and for a discussion of a possible particular relation through the methods of retrospect and symbolization see Herbert Edwards, "Henry James and Ibsen," *American Literature,* XXIV (1952), 208-223.

[14] *Scenic Art,* p. 258.

[15] *Ibid.,* p. 249.

[16] *Ibid.,* p. 245.

[17] *Ibid.,* p. 293; italics added.

[18] *The Notebooks of Henry James,* ed. F. O. Matthiessen and Kenneth B. Murdock (New York, 1955), p. 188. In the original context of the passage cited, the word "key" refers specifically to the use of a scenario; hereafter referred to as *Notebooks.*

[19] *Ibid.,* p. xviii.

[20] *Scenic Art,* p. 3.

[21] *Ibid.*

[22] *Prefaces,* p. 326.

[23] *Ibid.,* p. 318.

[24] *The Future of the Novel,* ed. Leon Edel (New York, 1956), pp. 9f; hereafter referred to as *Future.*

[25] *Prefaces,* p. 33.

[26] *Ibid.,* p. 34. There is a relation of correspondence between probability in the world of the novel and probability in the real world. The degree of this correspondence affects the coherence of events in the novel. It is this complex relation of internal and external verisimilitude that James touches on in the preface to *The American.*

[27] *Ibid.,* p. 114.

[28] *Ibid.* Perhaps James's most famous statement on the compact structure of the drama is the one now available in Edel's *Plays,* pp. 34f. Cf. *Notes,* p. 115, where James comments on structure in Balzac's novels.

[29] *Prefaces,* p. 112.

[30] *The Letters of Henry James,* ed. Percy Lubbock (New York, 1920), I, 176; hereafter referred to as Lubbock, *Letters.* The connection between dramatizing and seeing is poignantly stated by R. W. Short, "Some Critical Terms of Henry James," *PMLA,* LXV (1950), 668; hereafter referred to as "Terms." Also see Harold T. McCarthy, *Henry James, the Critical Process* (New York, 1958), Chs. I and III.

[31] *Prefaces,* p. 137.

[32] *French Poets and Novelists* (London, 1878), p. 224.

113

[33] *Prefaces*, p. 94. In relation to intensity and its representational dimension, it is interesting to note two passages in which James comments on Ibsen. Elizabeth Robins writes of James's attachment to Ibsen and quotes him in regard to the Norwegian playwright's "intensity, his vividness, the hard compulsion of his strangely inscrutable art." *Theatre and Friendship, Some Henry James Letters* (New York, 1932), p. 16. Yet in spite of this admiration of Ibsen, James shows himself abashed at the last act of *Little Eyolf*: "I fear, in truth, no harm *can* be done equal to the harm done to the play by its own most disappointing third act. . . . It seems to drop—dramatically, representably speaking; in short strangely and painfully meagre." *Ibid.*, p. 157.

[34] *Prefaces*, p. 256.

[35] Lubbock, *Letters*, I, 109.

[36] *Prefaces*, p. 56.

[37] *Ibid.*, p. 62. McCarthy remarks on this relation of Shakespeare's heroes to intensity that "with a hero of this kidney, the author could prepare for his reader a range of sensibility, a degree of intensity, that no amount of artistic solicitation could effect with such a one as Hyacinth Robinson." *Creative Process*, p. 72.

[38] *Prefaces*, p. 62.

[39] *Ibid.*, p. 129.

[40] *Ibid.*, p. 136.

[41] *Ibid.*, p. 138.

[42] *Ibid.*, p. 15.

[43] *Henry James and H. G. Wells, A Record of their Friendship, their Debate on the Art of Fiction and their Quarrel*, eds. Leon Edel and Gordon L. Ray (London, 1958), p. 57; hereafter referred to as *James and Wells*.

[44] Lubbock, *Letters*, I, 326.

[45] *Notes and Reviews*, preface by Pierre Chaignon La Rose (Massachusetts, 1921), p. 21.

[46] F. O. Matthiessen, *The American Renaissance* (New York, 1954), p. 280. Just previous to the sentence quoted Matthiessen had been discussing Hawthorne's "lapses from imaginative fitness," one of which was the narrator's personal intrusion in a description of Judge Pyncheon. This led him to remark that "the way that Hawthorne's intrusive notion robs his narrative of all sustained illusion at this point is the kind of thing James objected to most."

[47] Percy Lubbock, *The Craft of Fiction* (New York, 1957), p. 89; here-

after referred to as *Craft*. Richard Chase's observation of the dramatic quality of Faulkner's *The Sound and the Fury* is worth mention because that observation is, in the most rigid sense, Jamesian. He writes, "And we see that Faulkner has done in the Benjy section what every accomplished novelist has to be able to do. He eats his cake and has it too. That is, he establishes a character as his point of view; but Benjy as point of view is merely the dramatic convention of the piece. The actual point of view is still the author's, and his mind envelops the whole. The dramatic convention, however, is all-important and the Benjy section is a more accomplished piece of writing than it would be if the omniscient author were to appear merely as such." *The American Novel and Its Tradition* (New York, 1957), p. 226. Also, it should be noted that both Chase's and Lubbock's insistence on this dual author-character aspect of the novel makes James's statement that "the deepest quality of a work of art will always be the quality of the mind of the producer" perfectly consonant with his demand for objectivity.

[48] *James and Wells*, p. 174.

[49] *Prefaces*, p. 328.

[50] *Ibid.*, p. 144.

[51] *Ibid.*, p. 126. James quotes this as his original idea, but goes on to explain that space did not permit him to give it full treatment. Nevertheless, any reader of the novel will immediately note that Fleda Vetch's aesthetic and moral attitude toward the spoils distinguishes her from Mrs. Gereth, Owen, and Mona, each of whom has an attitude toward the spoils which becomes the earmark of his character in the novel.

[52] Lubbock, *Craft*, p. 196.

[53] *Prefaces*, pp. 110f.

[54] Lubbock, *Craft*, p. 150.

[55] *Prefaces*, p. 94.

[56] *Ibid.*, p. 257.

[57] *Ibid.*, p. 237.

[58] *Ibid.*, p. 87.

[59] Robins, pp. 209f.

[60] *Prefaces*, p. 278. The scenario was one means that James used to control the length of his fictions. The writing of the scenario as a preliminary and detailed sketch was, indeed, one of the greatest lessons that James learned during his theatrical career. It accounts for the strict organization evident in the novels of his post-theatrical period. There are scenarios in the notebooks for *Poynton*, *Maisie*, *Wings*, *Bowl*, and *The Am-*

bassadors. There is a brief but quite comprehensive note for *The Sacred Fount*; it is even possible that there was a scenario for it in notes of James's which are no longer extant. The preface to *The Awkward Age* cites a sketch that James prepared for his publisher before serialization of that novel. Leon Edel has informed me that he has been unable to find any trace of it. The sketch did, however, satisfy the editors of *Harper's Weekly.* We have, then, in the case of five major novels a scenario; in the case of the *Fount* an intelligible note; and in the case of the *Age* a sketch. The importance of the role of the scenario in the writing of this later fiction can hardly be questioned.

[61] Phyllis Bentley, *Some Observations on the Art of Narrative* (New York, 1947), p. 19.

[62] *The Twentieth Century Novel: Studies in Technique* (New York, 1932), p. 148.

[63] There is no attempt here to construct a "poetics" of the novel; nor any attempt to ape Aristotle. But, to be sure, there is an adapation of a well-established framework derived from the *Poetics*. Aristotle speaks of the means *in which* the poet imitates, and my discussion treats a significant aspect of James's language as the means of representation. Aristotle speaks of the action as the *object* imitated in the drama; my discussion treats the action as the subject represented (not imitated) in the dramatized novel. (See "Action," p. 19, and n. 71 below.) Aristotle distinguishes the *manner* of imitation via voice structure; my discussion treats aspects of the structure of a narrative in the mixed voice form by presenting scenes, pictures, and centres as macrostructures in the dramatized novel.

[64] More attention has been given to the imagery of James than to other stylistic considerations. Of the many articles see Robert L. Gale, "Freudian Imagery in James's Fiction," *American Imago,* XI (1954), 181-190; "Religion Imagery in Henry James's Fiction," *MFS,* III (1957), 64-72; "Art Imagery in Henry James's Fiction," *AL,* XXIX (1957), 47-63; Priscilla Gibson, "The Uses of James's Imagery: Drama through Metaphor," *PMLA,* LXIX (1954), 1076-1084; R. W. Short, "Henry James's World of Images," *PMLA,* LXVII (1953), 943-960; Austen Warren, "Henry James: Symbolic Imagery in the Later Novels," *Rage for Order: Essays in Criticism* (Chicago, 1948), pp. 142-161.

[65] The best study of James's style is, unfortunately, available on microfilm from Ann Arbor only. It is Leo T. Hendrick's "Henry James: The Late and Early Styles: A Stylistics Study." Also see Charles R. Crow, "The

Style of Henry James: *The Wings of the Dove,*" *Style in Prose Fiction,* ed. Harold C. Martin (New York, 1959), pp. 172-179, and R. W. Short, "The Sentence Structure of Henry James," *AL,* XVIII (1946), 71-88.

[66] *The Novels and Tales of Henry James : New York Edition* (New York, 1908), XI, 367f. All subsequent references will be to this volume and will be given in parentheses following the quotations.

[67] *Prefaces,* p. 181.

[68] I have been unable to locate any study which analyzes James's conception of action by collating numerous references to it in his work. Aspects of action, however, have been variously treated; see esp. Short, "Terms", n. 30; also Lubbock, *Craft,* Ch. XIII. My own interpretation of action is in basic agreement with Short's, though I would not, perhaps, emphasize the parallel with Aristotle as much as he does; rather I would be more inclined to see James deriving the action from his characters rather than vice versa. On this see Matthiessen, *The Major Phase* (New York, 1944), p. 181, and n. 71 below. Lubbock's splitting of action into internal and external serves its purpose, but it is hardly Jamesian; and the conversation the *Age* incorporates so frequently has reference to internal states that it impoverishes the novel to refer to it in terms of a purely external action.

[69] *Prefaces,* p. 182.

[70] *Notebooks,* p. 198.

[71] James's idea of action approximates but does not equate with Aristotle's. For Aristotle *praxis,* the action as a whole, is conceived as something outside of the literary structure. It is "the plot [*mythos*] which represents the action [*praxeos*]" for Aristotle, and by " 'plot' I mean here the arrangement of incidents [*pragmaton*]. . . ." 1450a8 in Hamilton Fyfe's trans. (London, 1946).

But James differs from Aristotle. He does not conceive of the novel primarily as an imitation of an action; rather it is a "direct impression of life" (*Future,* p. 9). When he speaks of action he refers to something which is within the structure of his novel. Therefore he writes of "the *action* embodied" in "In the Cage" (*Prefaces,* p. 157). This action does not seem to be the plot, "nefarious name, in any flash, upon the fancy, of a set of relations" (Prefaces, p. 42). It is true that at times James does equate plot and action; for instance, see *Partial Portraits,* pp. 105f. This, however, is unusual rather than usual with James. Thus the remarks of Herbert L. Hughes on this matter: "We find . . . that James believed firmly in form and finish and in what Poe called unity, or totality of effect, though I don't see that James thought of plot in the usual sense of it. Surely there was no outward complication of incident which he advocated as plot. Plot means a weaving together, and has so the connotation always been of a much tangled web, but James seems not to have thought of it, or spoken of the novel, in such terms," *Theory and Practice in Henry James* (Michigan, 1926), p. 35.

[72] *Notebooks*, p. 269.

[73] *Ibid.*, p. 348.

[74] *Ibid.*, p. 368.

[75] *The Selected Letters of Henry James*, ed. Leon Edel (New York, 1960), p. 190; hereafter referred to as *Selected Letters*.

[76] *Ibid.*, p. 206.

[77] *Notebooks*, p. 173.

[78] *Ibid.*, p. 174.

[79] *Prefaces*, p. 102.

[80] *Selected Letters*, p. 206.

[81] *Notebooks*, p. 227.

[82] *Ibid.*, p. 245.

[83] *Ibid.*, p. 197.

[84] *Ibid.*, p. 148.

[85] *Prefaces*, p. 157.

[86] *Ibid.*, p. 154.

[87] *Selected Letters*, pp. 202f.

[88] *Prefaces*, p. 16.

[89] *Ibid.*, pp. 56f.

[90] *Ibid.*, p. 128.

[91] *Ibid.*, p. 144.

[92] Short, "Terms," p. 669.

[93] *Prefaces*, p. 33.

[94] For discussions of the term "scene" as James used it, see Short, "Terms"; Beach, *Method*, pp. 72-79; Lubbock, esp. Ch. XIII; the most extensive treatment of scene is that of Douglas T. Bockes, "The Late Method of Henry James" (diss. Syracuse, 1954), pp. 16-70, which is available on microfilm.

[95] This, I presume, is Beach's meaning when he proposes that "The author of the novel must furnish his dialogue with full complement of setting and explanation," *Method*, p. 92, n. 2.

[96] *Selected Letters*, p. 149.

[97] *Prefaces*, p. 157.

[98] *Ibid.,* p. 323.

[99] *Notebooks,* p. 102.

[100] James describes the scene between Strether and Maria Gostrey in Bk. 2, Ch. 1 of *The Ambassadors* as "standard" in *Prefaces,* p. 323.

[101] *Prefaces,* p. 158.

[102] *The Ivory Tower,* ed. Percy Lubbock (London, 1917), p. 268. Dorothea Krook, "Principles and Method in the Later Works of Henry James," in *Interpretations of American Literature,* eds. Charles Feidelson, Jr. and Paul Brodkorb, Jr. (New York, 1959), pp. 267-271, discussed the law of successive Aspects in relation to the limitations of the protagonist, especially those deriving from pride and ennui. Also see Bockes, pp. 16-70, who treats Aspects in relation to scenes rather than in relation to reflectors.

[103] The conversation frequently borders on the stichomythic; Hendrick, p. 61.

[104] *Ibid.,* p. 57.

[105] *Craft,* p. 268.

[106] *Prefaces,* p. 323.

[107] The only readily available treatment of the term *picture* is Short's "Terms." Edwin T. Bowden offers a study of the pictorial nature of James's novels in *The Themes of Henry James: A System of Observation through the Visual Arts* (New Haven, 1956); for novel as picture see especially pp. 21f.

[108] I discuss two meanings of the word *picture*: (1) picture as a structural block which alternates with scene; (2) picture in the sense that a novel is an ordered composition. There at least two other uses of the word which I do not touch: (1) picture referring to the novel as a picture of life, a meaning which appears in a sentence remarking George Eliot's talent for producing "such rich, deep, masterly pictures of the multiform life of man," *Partial Portraits,* p. 62; (2) picture in the sense that the novel as a whole is a pictorial one; thus Lubbock on *The Ambassadors*: "It is a purely pictorial subject, covering Strether's field of vision and bounded by its limits; it consists entirely of an impression received by a certain man," *Craft,* p. 159.

[109] "The Style of Henry James," p. 181.

[110] *Notebooks,* p. 160.

[111] Lubbock approaches the summarized and related aspect of the picture when he writes: "When you recall and picture an impression in words you give us, listeners and readers, no more than the sight of things

in a mirror, not a direct view of them; but at the same time there is something of which you indeed give us a direct view, as we may say, and that is the mirror, your mind itself," *Craft,* p. 271.

[112] The notion of the variety of uses to which the picture is put is perhaps better represented by R. W. Short, who speaks of the law of the picture as "opportunistic." "Though James's pictures contain great life and, often, physical movements, they must perform their stint of representation in space rather than time. They must foreshorten, summarize, and withal give the effect of simultaneous representation," "Terms," p. 680. Hendrick, studying the late novels, gives statistical support to the stint of representation that the picture has to provide. In the 480-page segment he studied, he found "3470 sentences [of dialogue] in the early, 2558 in the late. It seems indisputable that the later fiction was more sparing of dialogue than the early," p. 48. He eventually goes on to remark that "the late dialogue carries less of its narrative than does the late non-dialogue," p. 69. The dialogue in the "late fiction is more concerned with defining what *has* happened than in relating what *will* happen. It focuses rather upon the gradual comprehension of a situation than upon a series of new situations," p. 57.

[113] Lubbock, *Letters,* I, 209.

[114] *Prefaces,* p. 263.

[115] *Ibid.,* p. 298. Insofar as James insisted on representation, on exhibition, be it ever so brief, it differed from what modern commentators refer to as summary: "Summary is that part of a novel in which the novelist says that things are happening, or that they have happened—and sometimes there is a prophetic summary at the end of the book about things that will happen." Robert Liddell, *Some Principles of Fiction* (London, 1953), pp. 62f. Also see Bentley, pp. 4-17.

[116] James has variously described foreshortening. It is a "figuring synthetically" (*Prefaces,* p. 88) that is designed to have "all the economy of picture" (*Ibid.,* p. 57); it imparts "to patches the value of presences" (*Ibid.,* p. 302). And there are indeed many other references to be found. The most comprehensive treatment of foreshortening to date is Morris Roberts, "Henry James and the Art of Foreshortening," *RES,* XXII (1946), 207-14. While the points Roberts makes are good ones, the treatment is too limited in its conception of foreshortening to be totally adequate. It does not, for instance, provide for James's remarks on "The Coxon Fund" (*Notebooks,* pp. 160-163) where he refers to the tale as

120

dramatized as well as summarized. And the latter word is rightly glossed by the editors (p. 163) as "foreshortened."

[117] Chapter X is composed of elements of dialogue and picture. It is difficult to determine which term—scene or picture—should designate it. James was aware of sequences of this sort in which "the boundary line between picture and scene bears a little the weight of double pressure" (*Prefaces*, p. 300). He once mentioned, in fact, "the odd inveteracy with which picture, at almost any turn, is jealous of drama, and drama . . . suspicious of picture" (*Ibid.*, p. 298). Without marring the terminology severely, it would seem acceptable to refer to a chapter like X as a scene, or at least scenic, since "to report at all closely and completely of what 'passes' on a given occasion is inevitably to become more or less scenic . . ." (*Ibid.*, p. 235).

[118] *Prefaces*, p. 158.

[119] *Ibid.*, p. 323.

[120] *Ibid.*, p. 158.

[121] *Ibid.*, p. 298. In speaking of scene and summary, description and summary, Phyllis Bentley remarks that they "are not proper antitheses. Though indeed—and this is the crux of the argument—the kinds of narrative described above are not antitheses, but distant points in a scale of subtle gradations, stretching from the specific to the integrated." *Some Observations*, p. 8.

[122] See E. M. Forster, *Aspects of the Novel* (New York, 1927), Ch. VIII, for an unsympathetic understanding of James on this point of the novel as a picture composed. Also see Beach, *Method*, pp. 24-37, which is more sympathetic and may have the further distinction of being the first discussion of James's novels as compositions.

[123] Taylor, p. 86.

[124] *Prefaces*, p. 84.

[125] *Selected Letters*, p. 158.

[126] On centres see esp. Short, "Terms"; also, Beach, *Twentieth Century Novel*, pp. 117-230; Lubbock, *Craft*, *passim*; additional discussions of merit are: Bockes, pp. 71-125; Francis Fergusson, "James's Idea of Dramatic Form," *KR*, V (1943), 495-507; Elizabeth L. Forbes, "Dramatic Lustrum: A Study of the Effect of Henry James's Theatrical Experience on His Later Novels," *NEQ*, XI (1938), 108-120; Taylor, pp. 48-56.

[127] *Prefaces*, p. 67.

[128] *Ibid.*, p. 101.

[129] *Craft,* p. 9.
[130] Taylor, p. 48.
[131] Tolstoi quoted in Walter Allen, *Writers on Writing* (New York, 1959), p. 147.
[132] *Prefaces,* p. 327.
[133] *Ibid.,* p. 15.
[134] *Ibid.,* pp. 34, 37f.
[135] *Ibid.,* p. 51.
[136] Clearly suggested by *Prefaces,* pp. 61f. and *passim* in same preface.
[137] *Ibid.,* p. 89.
[138] *Ibid.,* p. 110.
[139] Cf. Short, "Terms," p. 672.
[140] *Ibid.,* p. 317.
[141] For details on *The Golden Bowl* see Beach, *Twentieth Century Novel,* pp. 199-203.
[142] Caroline Gordon, *How to Read a Novel* (New York, 1957), pp. 96-110. Lubbock had used the term earlier in relation to Tolstoi; see *Craft,* p. 39.
[143] From his standard treatment of the matter—"Point of View in Fiction," *PMLA,* LXX (1955), 1160-1184—one can easily see that Norman Friedman does not admit this dichotomy. He and I, however, use different bases of classification. What Friedman lists as "Multiple Selective Omniscience," I call third person, external, and limited.
[144] Manuel Komroff, "View-Point," *Dictionary of World Literature* (New York, 1953), p. 439. Also see J. Craig La Drière, "Voice and Address," *Ibid.,* pp. 441-444. My basis of classification for types of points of view derives from these two studies.
[145] See Marius Bewley, *The Complex Fate* (New York, 1954), pp. 79-113.

CHAPTER 2

[1] Cf. *Prefaces,* p. 127.
[2] In *Poynton* James named his characters with characteristic care. *Fleda Vetch* is certainly an unflattering name for the heroine of any tale; yet it is one that James decided on after considerable brooding. Three years before he took up work on *Poynton,* he noted the name "Veitch (or Veetch)" in a notebook entry of December 27, 1892. In May of 1895,

when he began work on *The Old Things,* the novel's original title, James called the girl *Muriel Veech*—a name equally as unflattering as Fleda Vetch. While one might question why James bothered to change the name at all, it is certain that *Fleda,* a play on *fled,* is a name more compatible than *Muriel* with the flight imagery used to describe the heroine and her actions.

Mona is certainly a pun on *moaner*: moaning about Poynton is the girl's prime humor. It is relevant that James changed her Christian name from *Nora* to *Mona,* while retaining the surname *Brigstock.* The *brig* and the *stock* signal the confined area of sensibility in Mona. The name suggests a response which is as imaginative as Mona's home, *Waterbath.*

Mrs. Gereth's Christian name is Adela. It signals, as a variant of Adelaide, her nobility. It certainly fits the prerogatives of power and costly trappings to which she claims so absolute a right.

James changed her son's name from *Albert* to *Owen.* Perhaps, along with its noble associations, *Owen* also suggested to James an ironic contrast between that heroic doer of deeds Owen Glendower and the more hesitant Owen Gereth.

[8] Fleda is presented in relation to images of flight. "To know she had become to him an object of desire gave her wings that she felt herself flutter in the air . . ." (p. 105). When Owen tries to visit Fleda at her West Kensington residence, he finds that she has "flown" (p. 181). When he pursues her to Maggie's, Fleda realizes that she has "gained nothing by flight" (p. 182). Fleda finds a necessity, on one occasion, for "keeping cool and repressing a visible flutter" (p. 154). On another, she allows her generosity to "take . . . flight" (p. 108). Once she "felt the need moreover of taking breath after such a flight into the cold air of denial" (p. 121).

Fleda is much different from Mona. James seemed to see in Mona's feet a symbol of herself. They are quite big feet, and they are inevitably covered with highly glossed shoes: "Mona kept dropping her eyes, as she walked, to catch the sheen of her patent leather shoes, which resembled a man's and which she kicked forward a little . . . to help her to see what she thought of them" (p. 28). When Mona refuses to marry Owen without Poynton, Fleda muses: "Yes indeed she knew all she needed: all she needed was that Mona had proved apt at putting down that wonderful patent-leather foot" (p. 92). These and all subsequent quotations (with page citations in parentheses following quoted excerpts) are from *The Novels and Tales of Henry James: New York Edition* (New York, 1908), vol. X.

⁴ James uses Owen's teeth to indicate Fleda's danger: "Drawn into the eddy of the outpouring the girl, scared and embarrassed, laughed off her exposure; but only to feel herself more passionately caught up and, as it seemed to her, thrust down the fine open mouth (it showed such perfect teeth) with which poor Owen's slow cerebration gaped" (pp. 31f.). His indecision, hinted at above, seems quite evident in another "teeth" passage: ". . . Owen remained indistinct and on the whole unaggressive. He wouldn't be there with a cigarette in his teeth, very handsome and insolently quiet . . ." p. 56). But perhaps some of the attractiveness of Owen, although pictured ambiguously, is also found in his smile: ". . . A hansom pulled up short. . . . The occupant was exactly Owen Gereth, who . . . with an exhibition of white teeth that, from under the hood of the cab, had almost flashed through the fog, now alighted to ask her if he couldn't give her a lift" (p. 62).

⁵ Mrs. Gereth speaks of herself as Atlas "hunching up the back . . . under his globe" (p. 71).

⁶ For a more complete detailing of this imagery, see Alan H. Roper, "The Moral and Metaphorical Meaning of *The Spoils of Poynton*," *AL*, XXXII (1960), 183-190.

⁷ I find that my observations in this area of structural balance are paralleled by John Ciardi's work on Dante. His clear formulation of the phenomenon in the *Divine Comedy* has led me in two instances to paraphrase his remarks on what he calls *"back-illumination."* See "How to Read Dante," *Saturday Review* (June 3, 1961), p. 54.

⁸ *Ibid.*

⁹ *Prefaces,* p. 127.

¹⁰ Some critics feel that Fleda does not adhere to her principles. Among them are Yvor Winters, *In Defense of Reason* (New York, 1947), pp. 319f.; Patrick Quinn, "Morals and Motives in *The Spoils of Poynton*," *Sewanee Review,* LXII (1954), 563-577; and Edmond L. Volpe, "The Spoils of Art," *MLN,* LXXIV (1959), 601-608. Volpe (p. 607, n. 14) adequately dismisses Quinn's argument. His own brief against *Poynton,* which (knowingly or unknowingly) follows Winters, argues that the structure of the novel breaks down after Chapter XVI. He notes that Fleda sends a telegram recalling Owen after "Mrs. Gereth dominates Fleda intellectually" (p. 605), which should not happen. Fleda does not remain free; she is not "successful" (p. 607). "She forsakes the high prin-

NOTES

ciples that have guided her heroism and succumbs to the bribe" (p. 605).
She has a chance to get the spoils when Mrs. Gereth returns them, so she
succumbs to arguments and sends the telegram (p. 605). Richard Dankleff, in his monumental "The Composition, Revisions, Reception, and
Critical Reputation of Henry James's *The Spoils of Poynton*" (diss.
Chicago, 1959), pp. 18-20, holds that Fleda must help Mrs. Gereth now
because she sees her duty to Mrs. Gereth as greater than her duty to
Mona. He supports the argument (pp. 229f.) by listing and interpreting
the stylistic changes in the novel through its four editions. One can
argue and attain a satisfactory probability in this manner. I argued
similarly in an unpubl. diss. "The Moral Art of *The Spoils of Poynton*"
(U. of Detroit, 1958), pp. 50-54. There is, nevertheless, another argument which also has probability. One does not have to accept the major
premise of Winters and Volpe. A careful reading of the novel shows
that James was characteristically ambiguous. Fleda's assent to marrying
Owen can easily be argued as dependent on his freedom from Mona;
see "The Moral Art," pp. 54-57.
   [11] *Prefaces,* p. 127.
   [12] *Ibid.,* pp. 129f.
   [13] One cannot justify Fleda's action according to ordinary ethical standards wherein the end does not justify the means. But Fleda is, of course,
a pragmatist: her lying is justified by its service to Owen's honor. To
modern readers who tend to see this honor as more social than truly
human, Fleda loses stature as a heroine. But the integrity of *Poynton*
lies not with what the reader believes, but with what Fleda believes.
The case has been aptly put by D. W. Jefferson: "She is confronted with
a series of very intricate moral problems, which cannot be appreciated
unless they are seen also as emotional problems. That is, the point of
principle which guides Fleda cannot be safely isolated from its context
and considered abstractly. . . . Fleda's desire to be 'right' herself, and
her desire for Owen's rightness, are inseparable from her tender love for
him. It is an aspect of her love that it heightens her sense of pride in
high standards of behaviour," *Henry James* (New York, 1961), p. 70.
The reader who still finds Fleda wanting should turn to Oscar Cargill,
who points up the irony of her situation by juxtaposing the Maltese
Cross that Fleda wanted from Owen and the pincushion that she actually
got; *The Novels of Henry James* (New York, 1961), pp. 238-239.
   [14] "James the Old Intruder," *MFS,* IV (1958), 157-164.

CHAPTER 3

[1] *Notebooks,* p. 263.

[2] *Prefaces,* p. 149.

[3] *Ibid.,* p. 146.

[4] *Ibid.,* pp. 148f.

[5] James elaborated his relation to the centre of vision in the preface to the novel: "Small children have many more perceptions than they have terms to translate them; their vision is at any moment much richer, their apprehension even constantly stronger, than their prompt, their at all producible, vocabulary. Amusing therefore as it might at the first blush have seemed to restrict myself in this case to the terms as well as to the experience, it became at once plain that such an attempt would fail. Maisie's terms accordingly play their part—since her simpler conclusions quite depend on them; but our own commentary constantly attends and amplifies. This it is that on occasion, doubtless, seems to represent us as going so 'behind' the facts of her spectacle as to exaggerate the activity of her relation to them. The difference here is but of a shade: it is her relation, her activity of spirit, that determines all our own concern—we simply take advantage of these things better than she herself." *Prefaces,* pp. 145f.

[6] *Ibid.,* p. 145.

[7] *The Novels and Tales of Henry James: New York Edition* (New York, 1908), XI, 12f. All subsequent references will be to this volume and will be given in parentheses following the quotations.

[8] Bockes makes this same point: "Maisie's finer intelligence has really seen through to the center of the issue: the evil is not adultery but Sir Claude's enslavement to Mrs. Beale" ("The Late Method," p. 80). F. R. Leavis also circles this same point when he writes: "Her discriminations and judgments regard the qualities of personality and capacities for sensitive personal relations revealed by her adults as they perform the evolutions that are so largely set off by the spring of which she remains unaware. The 'moral sense' that Maisie can't produce for Mrs. Wix's satisfaction is the one that, in the world of *What Maisie Knew,* doesn't matter. The satire that plays upon it appeals for its positives to the sense defined in Maisie herself." See Leavis's discussion in Bewley's *Complex Fate,* p. 10. This, of course, does not represent the only interpretation that has been offered for *Maisie.* Harris W. Wilson, "What *Did* Maisie Know?" *CE,* XVII (1956), suggests that "What Maisie saw was

Sir Claude's sexual promiscuity, 'his Weakness,' and that the secret she discovered in Boulogne was that to win him for herself and Mrs. Wix, she must do battle with her stepmother in terms of that weakness. Her greatest asset opposed to Mrs. Beale's lush worldliness is her virginity, and that she is prepared to offer" (p. 281). Wilson concludes his interpretation by stating that if the novel is not what he makes it out to be, it is nothing but a "technical exercise" (p. 282). It seems quite obvious that Wilson ignores the whole area of value that critics like Leavis, Bewley, and Bockes have taken pains to elucidate. Consequently his interpretation is perhaps as complete a misreading of the novel as any that can be offered. Edward Wasiolek, "Maisie: Pure or Corrupt?" *CE,* XXII (1960), calls Wilson's "an improbable explanation" (p. 167). He suggests that "Standing in the shadow of adulthood, Maisie feels the first tremors of sex and self-interest. Maisie's intentions are still frank and honest; although in James's ambiguous art one might speculate that in her further advance into adulthood, self-interest may turn into selfish interests" (pp. 171f.). While one might question the probability of the arguments which lead to this conclusion (explicitly different from Bewley's, *Complex Fate,* p. 97), I think it more to the point to question the *relevance* of such a conclusion itself.

Oscar Cargill, *The Novels of Henry James,* pp. 256-258, however, supports Wilson's view, which he calls "conclusive." For him Wasiolek's theory is "too infantile in implication." Cargill seizes on James's phrase, "the death of her childhood," in support of Wilson: "It is to her [Maisie's] cynical sophistication, with its strange base in innocence, that James indubitably refers in his Preface, when he writes of the end of the book as 'the death of her childhood.' " In James's context, however, the phrase's rhetorical value changes: "Successfully to resist (to resist, that is, the strain of observation and the assault of experience) what would that be, on the part of so young a person, but to remain fresh, and still fresh, and to have even a freshness to communicate?—the case being with Maisie to the end that she treats her friends to the rich little spectacle of objects embalmed in her wonder. She wonders, in other words, to the end, to the death—the death of her childhood, properly speaking; after which (with the inevitable shift, sooner or later, of her point of view) her situation will change and become another affair, subject to other measurements and with a new centre altogether." *Prefaces,* pp. 146f. Maisie remains, in James's view, fresh throughout the novel. *A* shift in her point of view (not at all necessarily *the one* Wilson and Cargill hold to) will come "sooner or later," but not in *What Maisie Knew*. It seems to me enormously difficult to argue away Maisie's goodness; if anything, her innocence (infused with the type of recognition I argue for in this chapter) becomes virtue rather than cynicism or corruption. James seems to have seen it this way, too (in a passage to which neither Wilson nor Cargill give attention), when he wrote of Maisie's "really keeping the torch of virtue alive in an air tending infinitely to smother it; really in short making confusion worse confounded by drawing some stray fragrance of an ideal across the scent of selfishness, by sowing on barren strands, through the mere fact of presence, the seed of the moral life." *Prefaces*, p. 143. Thus, to make Maisie out, at the end of the novel, "as mature as Mrs. Beale," as Cargill does, seems to be to run in the face of James's announced intention, and even worse to destroy much of the novel's meaning and tone, which depend so largely on Maisie's becoming the opposite of what Mrs. Beale, Sir Claude and the Faranges stand for. There is good reason, then, to see the process of Maisie's maturity in a larger context than the one that sex alone provides for. As Cargill so graciously does, I refer the reader to D. W. Jefferson for a discussion of this larger context in his *Henry James*, pp. 72-75. Also, see James W. Gargano, *"What Maisie Knew*: the Evolution of a 'Moral Sense,' " *NCF*, XVI (1961), 44f.

[9] James emphasizes Mrs. Wix's role as moral guardian by assigning a name to her glasses—they are referred to as "straighteners" throughout the novel (pp. 26, 42, 236, 237, 244, 288, 317, 354), and they are trained on questionable relationships in order to make the true meaning of those relationships evident to Maisie.

[10] Bewley is apt in his comment on this point: "It is Maisie's mission in life (James is very clear about it) to educate her elders, but of the three people struggling for possession of Maisie in the concluding chapter, only poor old Mrs. Wix remains amenable to education," p. 101.

[11] There is a striking resemblance in James's procedure here with that of Balzac in, for instance, *Eugénie Grandet*, where one notes—after being exposed to the routine of Old Grandet's ways—how in the three or four pages (at the end of Chapter IV) the five years which cover the liquidation of Guillaume Grandet's debts are convincingly treated. James hadn't as Balzac did, recourse to the enmeshed habits of the French peasantry, but he had the acuteness to see the value of establishing customs where they were not strikingly enough a part of the *Sitz im Leben*. Thus he subjects Maisie to the ritual of the changing of parents,

which adequately signals the passing of years in a few paragraphs.

[12] My discussion of economy in *Maisie* owes much to Henry L. Terrie, Jr., "Henry James and the Explosive Principle," *NCF*, XV (1961), p. 284, where he suggests five methods of economic presentation that James employs in his novels.

[13] Leavis singles out this event for discussion: *Complex Fate*, pp. 129f.

[14] Bockes remarks, "This kind of triple point of view—*i.e.*, Maisie's, the reader's view of Maisie, and the reader's view of Maisie's knowledge—makes for the greatest intensity of expression," p. 75.

[15] There is one blatant exception to this generalization, which occurs on pp. 281f., where the "Old Intruder" makes his presence inartistically felt.

Chapter 4

[1] *Prefaces*, pp. 109ff.

[2] *Ibid.*, p. 110.

[3] *Ibid.*, p. 106. Cargill, following a lead in James's Preface, relates the dialogue structure of the *Age* to the work of Gyp and Levedan; see *The Novels of Henry James*, pp. 263f.

[4] *Prefaces*, pp. 110f.

[5] Beach, *Method*, pp. 243-245, and Lubbock, *Craft*, pp. 188-202, elaborate some of the mechanics of a novel which approximates a play.

[6] *The Novels and Tales of Henry James : New York Edition* (New York, 1908), IX, 44-46. All subsequent references will be to this volume and will be given in parentheses following the quotations.

[7] This description of Brookenham, like many other descriptions in the novel, is uncomfortably close to the character sketches that playwrights like Shaw and Barrie use in their dramas. James, in imitating the play, went so far as to include in his novel those parts of the play (the sketches) which disappear—or rather appear in another form (tone, action, gesture, etc.)—when the play is acted. For those interested, F. W. Dupee, *Henry James: His Life and Writings* (New York, 1956), pp. 171f., presents a more sympathetic view of the assimilation of theatrical techniques to the novel form.

[8] F. R. Leavis cleverly argues that James wants his reader to be annoyed by the conversations of his characters: "Actually, the various ways in which we are to feel about the various characters are delicately but surely defined; and the whole point of the book depends upon our feel-

ing a strong distaste for some of the characters. . . ." *The Great Tradition* (New York, 1954), p. 206. He qualifies his statement, though, when he remarks, "Nevertheless, perhaps even *The Awkward Age,* brilliant success as it is, represents a disproportionate amount of 'doing,' a disproportionate interest in technique," *ibid.,* p. 207. The final point which he makes on the technique pinpoints the unrest that a reader feels with the novel: "And the reading that *The Awkward Age* exacts is . . . too intensively and predominantly a matter of 'wits,' in a limiting sense, to permit of the profoundest and most massive imaginative effect," *ibid.,* p. 208.

⁹ *Craft,* pp. 191f. J. A. Ward takes a rather larger view than Lubbock's as to the subject of the novel—a view of the kind that might enable him to quarrel with some of my censures of the novel. See *The Imagination of Disaster: Evil in the Fiction of Henry James* (Nebraska, 1961), pp. 90ff.

¹⁰ I haven't found any critic who has come to view *The Awkward Age* in exactly this manner. For F. R. Leavis, "*The Awkward Age,* though it exhibits James's genius for social comedy at its most brilliant, is a tragedy; a tragedy conceived in an imagination that was robustly, delicately and clairvoyantly moral," *Great Tradition,* p. 207. Joseph Firebaugh elaborates on the moral interest by connecting it with pragmatism ("attempting to discover the value of an idea by examining its effect on human life," p. 433) and "the fable of the fall of man" ("the conflict of knowledge *vs.* innocence, good *vs.* evil, or, to use more civilized terminology, realities *vs.* conventions," p. 426), "The Pragmatism of Henry James," *Virginia Quarterly Review,* XXVII (1951). For Ezra Pound the *Age* is "a study in punks, a cheese *soufflé* of the leprous crust of society done to a turn and a niceness save where he puts on the *dolcissimo, vox humana* stop," Literary Essays of Ezra Pound, ed. T. S. Eliot (London, 1954), p. 323. The opposite of this view is represented by F. W. Dupee: "The social entity is more literally the hero than in any of the novels. Superficially the book is satire at the expense of fashionable London . . ." *Henry James,* p. 172. The latest interpretation of the novel, Robert Marks, *James's Later Novels* (New York, 1960), pp. 15-43, deserves mention but cannot be conveniently summarized.

¹¹ If the use of Van's French novel reflects anything, it reflects a device of the well-made play. The use of the French novel to knit together incidents and to focus attention in a scene is a type of stagecraft which has its exemplar in the fan of Wilde's *Lady Windermere.*

CHAPTER 5

[1] Wilson Follett sees the *Fount* as "James's definitive parable of life and the artist" and as "one of the most stupendous parodies ever concocted . . .": "Henry James's Portrait of Henry James," *New York Times Book Review* (August 22, 1936), pp. 2, 16. R. P. Blackmur views the *Fount* as a study in human relationships, and he connects it with the tradition of James's ghostly tales: "The Sacred Fount," *KR*, IV (1942), 328-352. Claire J. Raeth associates the method of the *Fount* with James's short stories and views it as a failure in light of them: "Henry James's Rejection of *The Sacred Fount*," *ELH*, XVI (1949), 308-324. Leon Edel wrote the introductory essay to the Grove Press edition of the *Fount* in 1953. In it he examines the vampire theme, appearance and reality, the tradition of ambiguity in James and the novel's connection with what he considers James's idea of "sex as a depleting force." His is the first essay to establish on literary grounds that the *Fount* "as a technical performance [is] a masterpiece of the story-teller's art." Robert A. Perlongo calls the *Fount* "as close to autobiography as James ever came in a work of fiction"; he also sees the novel as a parable, "as a kind of psychological detective story," and as a "twentieth-century approximation of a Greek tragedy": "*The Sacred Fount*: Labyrinth or Parable?" *KR*, XXII (1960), 635-647. Ralph Ranald sees in the *Fount* "a theory of art and a theory of morality and a theory of love"; for him, primarily, the novel deals in the vampiristic and exposes the false artist: "*The Sacred Fount*: James's Portrait of the Artist *Manqué*, *NCF*, XV (1960), 239-248. Norma Phillips gives a new turn to the vampire theme and sees the narrator as the last victim: "Mrs. Brissenden's growth in subtle awareness and in fineness of perception, to the point where she can even turn these newly acquired weapons against her teacher, is achieved by her having filled her receptacle at the sacred fount of his acute consciousness." She views the novel, consequently, as the narrator's "self-destructive drama": "*The Sacred Fount*: The Narrator and the Vampires," *PMLA*, LXXVI (1961), 407-412. Oscar Cargill also calls the novel a "bizarre tragedy of self-destruction," but views its ultimate value more as propaedeutic than otherwise: "If *The Sacred Fount* is regarded as a sort of preliminary try at the stuff of *The Ambassadors*, its significance in James's development is greatly enlarged," *Novels of Henry James*, p. 295. Landon Burns sees the theme as "a discussion of the correspondence between life and art": "Henry James's Mysterious Fount," *Texas Studies in Literature and*

Language, II (1961), 520-528. James Folsom returns to the vampire theme and views the narrator as the chief vampire; the *Fount* is seen as a "parable of truth told by the father of lies"; James's narrator, he holds, is "like Archimago": "Archimago's Well: An Interpretation of *The Sacred Fount,*" *MFS,* VIII (1961), 136-144.

² Ezra Pound writes: "In *The Sacred Fount* he attains form, perfect form, his form. . . . It seems to me to be one work that he could afford to sit back, look at and find completed," *Literary Essays,* p. 327. For Charles G. Hoffman "*The Sacred Fount* borders on the formless," *The Short Novels of Henry James* (New York, 1957), p. 104.

³ *The Sacred Fount,* intro. by Leon Edel (New York, 1953), p. 1. Subsequent quotations, with page citations given in the parentheses following excerpts, are from this edition.

⁴ The case of Ford Obert's noticing Guy's age was already cited. In Ch. II, p. 22, the narrator's dinner partner corroborates the fact that Grace looks young.

⁵ A very casual reading of their essays will show that Follett and Perlongo base their interpretations on this theory. Ranald and Burns do not base theirs directly on the reliability of Mrs. Brissenden, but it is evident that they are more inclined to accept her view of the situation than the narrator's.

⁶ This is Follett's theory.

⁷ See p. 307. For the narrator, Mrs. Brissenden's invitation (prior to her having, as she professes, information from her husband) could be interpreted only as the result of anxiety to protect Long.

⁸ See p. 264.

⁹ Perlongo reads "tone" here as Grace Brissenden's "sense of reality." He comes to this conclusion, however, in face of the most glaring textual difficulties. When (on p. 318) Grace asks the narrator, "Then what on earth *do* you think?" he relates: "The strange mixture in my face naturally made her ask it, but everything, within a minute, had somehow so given way under the touch of her supreme assurance, the presentation of her own now finished system, that I dare say I couldn't at the moment have in the least trusted myself to tell her. She left me, however, in fact, small time—she only took enough, with her negations arrayed and her insolence recaptured, to judge me afresh, which she did as she gathered herself up into the strength of twenty-five."

¹⁰ Hoffman objects to the *Fount,* as a matter of fact, for being too concerned with the narrator's mind; he concludes that the novel is not dra-

matic because "the central situation . . . is *talked about* (not dramatically presented) in the novel." He sees the central situation to be that "one partner extracts 'new blood' at the other partner's expense," p. 104. But, of course, this is not the central situation at all. The drama takes place on the stage of the narrator's consciousness rather than on the grounds of Newmarch. As far as the controlling ambiguity allows, the action of "making things fit," in which both the narrator and Mrs. Brissenden engage, is as dramatic as it could be.

[11] The narrator is no paragon of virtue, certainly; but the now popular attempt to make him the arch-villain of Newmarch seems somewhat naive. Ranald makes the narrator another Roger Chillingworth (*NCF,* XV, 245), and Folsom somewhat carelessly writes that the narrator "feeds on several victims . . . drawing life-blood from each." For him, "A vampire is a man who uses his mind to feed off someone else" (*MFS,* VIII, 140f.). Both Ranald and Folsom fail to distinguish between an observer and a vampire. They fail to see that the narrator's activity does not deplete those whom he observes. And both writers fail to remember that what they term "vampirism" is the type of activity repeatedly recorded in James's *Notebooks.* The conclusion is obvious.

[12] Throughout the novel there is an emphasis on building, the idea of making things fit, and the artistic process.

[13] See Beach, *Method,* p. 44.

[14] There is an evident danger in pursuing comparisons of this type too far. The purpose of introducing the musical one here, however, is to give a notion of how the novel's "movement" takes place; it provides, in other words, a helpful analogy. I have no evidence that James intended to model his novel on a double fugue, but regardless of this fact, there is in evidence in the novel a structure which seems easily understood in the light of that of a fugue.

The comments on the structure of the fugue itself derive from Percy A. Scholes, "Fugue Form," *The Oxford Companion to Music* (London, 1955), pp. 376-379.

[15] Cf. Beach, *Method,* pp. 250-254.

[16] *Criticism in American Periodicals of the Works of Henry James from 1866-1916* (Washington, D. C., 1944), pp. 80-82.

[17] *Henry James,* p. 171. Oscar Cargill registers a strong reaction to the title Dupee assigned to that section of his book which treats the novels under discussion: ". . . The epithet applied by F. W. Dupee, 'the awkward period,' to this passage in his work is one of the most gratuitous

of critical blunders, confuted by the very attention, in the main, that Dupee gives to it. Save for *The Sacred Fount,* possibly, who would wish one of these novels unwritten? They not only helped Henry James to increase his skill for the major tasks ahead of him, but they have taught two generations to understand and appreciate technique in the novel, and thus prepared the way for the comprehension of modern fiction, unappreciable to some degree without an instructed taste," *The Novels of Henry James,* p. 296.

Selective Bibliography

James, Henry. *The Novels and Tales of Henry James: New York Edition.* New York: Charles Scribner's Sons, 1908.

    Vol. IX. *The Awkward Age.*

        X. *The Spoils of Poynton. A London Life. The Chaperon.*

        XI. *What Maisie Knew. In the Cage. The Pupil.*

——. *The Sacred Fount.* New York: Grove Press, 1953.

——. *The Art of the Novel: Critical Prefaces.* Ed. R. P. Blackmur. New York: Charles Scribner's Sons, 1957.

——. *The Complete Plays of Henry James.* Ed. with intro. Leon Edel. Philadelphia: J. B. Lippincott, 1949.

——. *French Poets and Novelists.* London: Macmillan, 1878.

——. *The Future of the Novel.* Ed. Leon Edel. New York: Vintage Books, 1956.

——. *Henry James and H. G. Wells, A Record of their Friendship, their Debate on the Art of Fiction and their Quarrel.* Ed. Leon Edel and Gordon L. Ray. London: Hart-Davis, 1958.

——. *The Letters of Henry James.* 2 vols. Ed. Percy Lubbock. New York: Charles Scribner's Sons, 1920.

——. *The Notebooks of Henry James.* Ed. F. O. Matthiessen and Kenneth B. Murdock. New York: George Braziller, Inc., 1955.

——. *Notes and Reviews.* Ed. Pierre Chaignon La Rose. Massachusetts: Dunster House, 1921.

——. *Notes on Novelists.* London: J. M. Dent and Sons, 1914.

——. *The Scenic Art, Notes on Acting and Drama: 1872-1901.* Ed. Allan Wade. New York: Hill and Wang, 1957.

——. *The Selected Letters of Henry James.* Ed. Leon Edel. New York: Doubleday, 1960.

——. *Theatre and Friendship, Some Henry James Letters.* Ed. with commentary Elizabeth Robins. New York: G. P. Putnam's Sons, 1932.

Beach, Joseph Warren. *The Method of Henry James.* Philadelphia: Albert Saifer, 1954.

——. *The Twentieth Century Novel: Studies in Technique.* New York: Appleton-Century-Crofts, 1932.

Bentley, Phyllis. *Some Observations on the Art of Narrative.* New York: Macmillan, 1947.

Bewley, Marius. *The Complex Fate.* New York: Grove Press, 1954.

Blackmur, R. P. "The Sacred Fount," *Kenyon Review*, IV (1942), 328-352

Bockes, Douglas T. "The Late Method of Henry James." Syracuse: Unpub. diss., 1954.

Bowden, Edwin T. *The Themes of Henry James: A System of Observation through the Visual Arts*. New Haven: Yale University Press, 1956.

Brebner, Adele. "How to Know Maisie," *College English*, XVII (1956), 283-285.

Broderick, John C. "Nature, Art, and Imagination in *The Spoils of Poynton*," NCF, XIII (1959), 295-312.

Burns, Landon. "Henry James's Mysterious Fount," *Texas Studies in Literature and Language*, II (1961), 520-528.

Cargill, Oscar. *The Novels of Henry James*. New York: Macmillan, 1961.

Ciardi, John. "How to Read Dante," *Saturday Review* (June 3, 1961), 12-14, 53-54.

Crews, Frederick C. *The Tragedy of Manners: Moral Drama in the Late Novels of Henry James*. New Haven: Yale University Press, 1957.

Crow, Charles R. "The Style of Henry James: *The Wings of the Dove*," *Style in Prose Fiction*. Ed. Harold C. Martin. New York: Columbia University Press, 1959.

Dankleff, Richard. "The Composition, Revisions, Reception, and Critical Reputation of Henry James's *The Spoils of Poynton*." Chicago: Unpubl. diss., 1959.

Dupee, F. W. *Henry James: His Life and Writings*. New York: Doubleday, 1956.

Edel, Leon. "Introduction," *The Sacred Fount*. New York: Grove Press, 1953.

Edwards, Herbert. "Henry James and Ibsen," *AL*, XXIV (1952), 208-223.

Fergusson, Francis. "James's Idea of Dramatic Form," *Kenyon Review*, V (1943), 495-507.

Firebaugh, Joseph. "The Pragmatism of Henry James," *Virginia Quarterly Review*, XXVII (1959), 419-435.

Foley, Richard. *Criticism in American Periodicals of the Works of Henry James from 1866-1916*. Washington, D. C.: Catholic University of America Press, 1944.

Follett, Wilson. "Henry James's Portrait of Henry James," *New York Times Book Review* (August 23, 1936), 2, 16.

Folsom, James. "Archimago's Well: An Interpretation of *The Sacred Fount*," *MFS*, VIII (1961), 136-144.

Forbes, Elizabeth L. "Dramatic Lustrum: A Study of the Effect of Henry James's Theatrical Experience on His Later Novels," *New England Quarterly*, XI (1938), 108-120.

Forster, E. M. *Aspects of the Novel*. New York: Harcourt, Brace, 1927.

Gale, Robert L. "Freudian Imagery in James's Fiction," *American Imago*, XI (1954), 181-190.

———. "Religion Imagery in Henry James's Fiction," *MFS*, III (1957), 64-72.

———. "Art Imagery in Henry James's Fiction," *AL*, XXIX (1957), 47-63.

Gargano, James W. *What Maisie Knew*: the Evolution of a 'Moral Sense,' " *NCF*, XVI (1961), 33-46.

Gibson, Priscilla. "The Uses of James's Imagery: Drama through Metaphor," *PMLA*, LXIX (1954), 1076-1084.

Hendrick, Leo T. "Henry James: The Late and Early Styles: A Stylistics Study." University of Michigan: Unpubl. diss., 1953.

Hoffman, Charles G. *The Short Novels of Henry James*. New York: Twayne, 1957.

Hughes, Herbert L. *Theory and Practice in Henry James*. Michigan: Edwards Brothers, 1926.

Jefferson, D. W. *Henry James*. New York: Grove Press, 1961.

Krook, Dorothea. "Principles and Method in the Later Works of Henry James," *Interpretations of American Literature*. Ed. Charles Feidelson, Jr. and Paul Brodkorb, Jr. New York: Oxford University Press, 1959.

Leavis, F. R. *The Great Tradition*. New York: Doubleday, 1954.

———. "*What Maisie Knew*: A Disagreement by F. R. Leavis," Marius Bewley, *The Complex Fate*. New York: Grove Press, 1954.

Levy, Leo B. *Versions of Melodrama: A Study of the Fiction and Drama of Henry James, 1865-1897*. Berkeley: University of California Press, 1957.

Liddell, Robert. *A Treatise on the Novel*. London: Jonathan Cape, 1947.

———. *Some Principles of Fiction*. London: Jonathan Cape, 1953.

Lubbock, Percy. *The Craft of Fiction*. New York: Viking Press, 1957.

Marks, Robert. *James's Later Novels.* New York: William-Frederick Press, 1960.

Matthiessen, F. O. *The Major Phase.* New York: Oxford University Press, 1944.

McCarthy, Harold T. *Henry James: the Creative Process.* New York: Thomas Yoseloff, 1958.

Perlongo, Robert A. "*The Sacred Fount:* Labyrinth or Parable?," *Kenyon Review,* XXII (1960), 635-647.

Phillips, Norma. "*The Sacred Fount:* The Narrator and the Vampires," *PMLA,* LXXVI (1961), 407-412.

Pound, Ezra. *Literary Essays of Ezra Pound.* Ed. T. S. Eliot. London: Faber and Faber, 1954.

Quinn, Patrick. "Morals and Motives in *The Spoils of Poynton,*" *Sewanee Review,* LXII (1954), 563-577.

Raeth, Claire J. "Henry James's Rejection of *The Sacred Fount,*" *ELH,* XVI (1949), 308-324.

Ranald, Ralph. "*The Sacred Fount:* James's Portrait of the Artist Manqué," *NCF, XV* (1960), 239-248.

Roberts, Morris. "Henry James and the Art of Foreshortening," *RES,* XXII (1946), 207, 214.

Roper, Alan H. "The Moral and Metaphysical Meaning of *The Spoils of Poynton,*" *AL,* XXXII (1960), 182-196.

Short, R. W. "Some Critical Terms of Henry James," *PMLA,* LXV (1950), 667-680.

——. "Henry James's World of Images," PMLA, LXVII (1953), 943-960.

——. "The Sentence Structure of Henry James," *AL,* XVIII (1946), 71-88.

Snell, Edwin Marion. *The Modern Fables of Henry James.* Cambridge, Mass.: Harvard University Press, 1935.

Taylor, Christy Morgan. "The Pictorial Element in the Theory and Practice of Henry James." Stanford: Unpubl. diss., 1955.

Terrie, Jr., Henry L. "Henry James and the Explosive Principle," *NCF,* XV (1961), 283-299.

——. "Pictorial Method in the Novels of Henry James." Princeton: Unpubl. diss., 1955.

Tilford, John. "James the Old Intruder," *MFS,* IV (1958), 157-164.

Volpe, Edmond L. "The Spoils of Art," *MLN,* LXXIV (1959), 601-608.

Ward, J. A. *The Imagination of Disaster: Evil in the Fiction of Henry*

James. Nebraska: University of Nebraska Press, 1961.

Warren, Austin. *Rage for Order: Essays in Criticism*. Chicago: University of Chicago Press, 1948.

Wasiolek, Edward. "Maisie, Pure or Corrupt?" *College English*, XXII (1960), 167-172.

Wellek, Rene. "Henry James's Literary Theory and Criticism," *AL*, XXX (1958), 293-321.

Wilson, Harris W. "What *Did* Maisie Know?" *College English*, XVII (1956), 279-282.

Winters, Yvor. *In Defense of Reason*. New York: Swallow Press, 1947.

Worden, Ward S. "A Cut Version of *What Maisie Knew*," *AL*, XXIV (1953), 493-504.

Wyld, Lionel. "Drama vs. Theater in Henry James," *Four Quarters*, VII (1958), 17-26.